THE EVERYDAY AIR FRYER RECIPE BOOK

A Delicious Collection of Quick, Easy and Cost-Effective Recipes
For the Whole Family and Busy People

From Breakfast to Dinner
Incl. Snacks, Rice and Desserts

Lily Byrne

TABLE OF CONTENT

Introduction

An air fryer is an appliance that allows food to be fried by exploiting the high temperatures reached in the cooking chamber, without the need to heat the oil for frying.

The air fryer is a very versatile tool, especially if you have little time to cook and don't want to get dirty all over.

And it is also very useful to avoid having the unpleasant smell of fried food that fills the whole house.

The air fryer works like a small oven, so it lends itself very well to all those cooking that require dry heat. In practice, roasted or breaded dishes of meat or fish are very well prepared, but it is not suitable for steam cooking or for preparing boiled dishes.

It is perfect for frozen or pre-fried preparations, such as those found in the supermarket. But it is even better to prepare lighter versions of delicious dishes that are normally cooked fried, but with little fat.

The air fryer also works very well with vegetables, especially those that are usually grilled. And it is also great for cooking potatoes, both fried and baked.

Furthermore, since it works like a small oven, you can even bake bread in it, or use it for preparations with puff pastry.

Finally, it's a great quick way to reheat leftover food, especially if it needs to come back crisp.

Launched on the market for the first time by the Philips Electronics Company, the air fryer is a small appliance that, mimicking the operation of a normal convection oven, promises fried-like dishes with reduced fat content.

The operation of the air fryer is allowed by its special cooking chamber.

Usually in oil fryers, or in cooking that involves heating the oil at high temperatures for cooking, the hot oil is precisely the vector that allows food to be cooked.

In the air fryer, it is not necessary to use oil at high temperatures to be able to cook food, as it is the air itself that is used as a cooking vector.

In order to achieve homogeneous cooking, the hot air is cycled at extremely high rates to mimic the way oil behaves during traditional frying.

The meal must be thoroughly submerged in boiling oil when traditional frying is used. Food cooked in a hot air fryer is surrounded by a heat carrier, which causes the food to crisp up on the surface and soften on the inside.

The air fryer uses convection to cook, which means that it spins hot air into a vortex, much like a tiny, extremely potent ventilated oven.

It is possible to raise the temperature of the hot air to around 200 °C.

Advantages of using an air fryer

What are the benefits of using the air fryer? Below you will find a list of all the advantages that you will find in using the air fryer compared to traditional frying.

➤ Healthier food cooking. There is no need to use a lot of oil to get crunchy and well browned foods. Most people just sprinkle a little oil on the food to be cooked and then proceed to the cooking cycle. The hot air takes advantage of the little oil, and the excess oil is eliminated from the food. Furthermore, unlike a traditional oven, air frying is cooked faster and excess oil does not infiltrate the food.

➤ Faster cooking. Air fryers are usually faster than traditional ovens, especially when it comes to the time it takes to preheat.

➤ Easy to use. Air fryers are anything but complicated. They don't have dozens of options, just basic controls, which are simple to understand and use.

➤ Perfect for reheating food. Unlike microwaves that make food to be heated chewy or hard and traditional ovens, which make it dry, the air fryer heats food while maintaining its natural consistency.

➤ Makes cleaning faster. You will not have splashes of fat all over your cooking perimeter. The only parts of the air fryer that need cleaning are the basket and drawer because everything is contained inside of it.

➤ In this way, you will also save time for long-term cleaning because you will not have accumulations of grease inside your ventilation hood.

Tips for a better use

To use the air fryer perfectly, you need to know some basic rules.

• First, remember that most air fryers need to be preheated. It is a fundamental step and servings to ensure uniform cooking, so do not skip it.

• Regardless of the meal, lubricate the air fryer basket with a little oil to prevent the food from sticking during cooking. A creative technique is to use a spray canister to produce a thin and uniform veil.

• Evaluate, based on the model you have, how many people you can cook and or how much weight in ingredients. It is information that you usually find directly on the packaging or in the instructions. In any case, you prefer to cook more to avoid overloading the basket.

- If you want to cook foods covered with batter, make sure that the batter or breading is well attached to the food otherwise it risks coming off the basket during cooking.
- Before cooking wet foods, to avoid problems during cooking, it is advisable to grease the inside of the cooking chamber with a napkin soaked in oil. This step is also very useful when cleaning the fryer.
- To ensure that your food is perfectly cooked, remember to move the basket from time to time or turn the food halfway through cooking.
- Spray oil at mid-cooking. Spraying the oil halfway through cooking results in greater crunchiness on most foods.
- Read the instructions carefully. The first thing you need to do when buying an air fryer is to read the instructions carefully. In some models, you can find them directly in the package. Others, however, plan to download a smartphone application or connect to the manufacturer's website. In any case, never skip this step. It is essential to know your product to understand how to use it, how to clean it, and how to make it last longer.
- Remember to let the air fryer cool down properly. Once finished using it, the air fryer should be allowed to cool before being put to wash or hand washed. This argument is very valid, especially for those models that are made of plastic on the outside. If not allowed to cool to room temperature, in fact, they risk breaking.

Tips for a healthier use

Due to the expanding health benefits of this cooking technique and the on-going demand for fried meals, air fryers have recently experienced a boom in popularity.

Manufacturers of air fryers promote their product as a safe and efficient way to prepare and enjoy fried dishes. Dishes that are air-fried have less fat than foods that are deep-fried, making them healthier.

To get all the health benefits of the air fryer there are some tips you need to follow.

- Using too many added fats, such as oils or butter. The air fryer requires little oil to obtain certain external consistencies. For most foods, 1/2 teaspoon will suffice.
- Ignore the smoke point of the oil used. The smoke point is the maximum temperature that an oil or fat can reach before it begins to burn and generate toxic substances. Some commonly used oils have smoke points well below the temperature you are sure to set your fryer too, so they are not suitable for this application. In this sense, avocado, peanut, sesame, safflower, and sunflower oils are better suited, but olive oil (not extra virgin) is also fine.
- Allow dirt and grease to accumulate. Although little or no oil is required when using an air fryer, dirt and grease can still accumulate. Considering that the deep fryer can get very hot, these build-ups could cause burns, contaminate meals, or make cleaning very difficult. Remember that the air fryer should be cleaned after each use.

- Do not give the air fryer adequate space. Since air fryers are essentially small versions of ventilated mode ovens, they require space and ventilation during use. The advice is to dedicate an appropriate space to it, to allow the flow of air around the device, and place it on a stable and heat-resistant surface.
- Never dry out the food. The biggest enemy of air frying is moisture since it causes food to steam and lessens its crispness. So, it is suggested to pat dry with a piece of paper towel in order to promote browning.
- It is important to turn the meat during cooking. A common mistake is not to overturn foods such as meat. It must be done halfway through cooking so that the meat is well cooked on both sides. And for those unevenly thick pieces, like pork fillets or fish fillets, the thinner pieces need to be doubled to equal size and ensure even cooking.
- Never use spray oils. This is because spray oils ruin the accessories and the inside of the air fryer. Aerosol cans have aggressive agents that do not match the lining of most air fryer baskets.

How to handle frozen food

As you understand, you can cook in the air fryer both foods prepared by you, both frozen and pre-fried frozen foods such as French fries.

Remember that cooking times and temperatures vary according to the amount of food and the type of frozen food you intend to cook.

> For proper cooking, remember to never defrost foods that will then be cooked in the air fryer.

Also, for even and crisp cooking, remember to grease the air fryer basket with a little oil before cooking your frozen foods.

When placing frozen foods in the basket, remember that it is better not to stack them, to cook them well and evenly.

How to clean and maintain

As with all the appliances we have at home, even the air fryer requires proper maintenance to remain efficient for a long time.

It is therefore necessary to take care of the air fryer even with proper cleaning.

Among the advantages of the air fryer, is that the basket in which you cook can be removed and washed in the dishwasher.

The basket, however, is not the only element of this appliance that needs to be cleaned.

The first rule to follow to clean your air fryer well is to wait until it has cooled down.

As for the basket, as we have already said, it can be safely washed in the dishwasher.

In general, before putting the basket in the dishwasher, it is good practice to clean the bottom by collecting the dirt or oil that has drained to have the basket as clean as possible.

If there are encrustations or grease stains, you can proceed with a soak, with a little soap and water, for about 30 minutes, then clean up and then put to wash.

Once the basket has been removed, the heating element must also be cleaned. To clean the heating element, proceed as follows: remove the basket, overturn the air fryer and, with a sponge moistened with water and very little soap, proceed to clean it slowly.

You can also use water with a little lemon or vinegar. Also in this case, like the basket, the resistance must be cold. And then it must be dried well.

Especially if you have cooked food such as fish, bad smells may remain in the air fryer, and you can use lemon to remove them. Just cut it in half and rub it inside the basket, leave it to act for 30 minutes, then rinse and then dry carefully.

A valid alternative, if the smells do not go away, is this. Put a solution consisting of one part of vinegar and five parts of water on the bottom of the basket, without the grid. Then turn on the air fryer at 180-200 ° C and let this solution cook until it has almost completely evaporated.

Remember that, even if it is an excellent ally in the kitchen, especially for the most stubborn dirt, the spray degreaser must never be used to clean the air fryer. First, because it is very aggressive and risks ruining the pieces, especially the external part. The second reason is that the chemicals it is made of are too strong and risk not being properly rinsed by the various components of the air fryer, especially the internal ones.

Cooking time chart

Below you will find a list of the main foods to cook in the air fryer. The times and cooking times are in any case relative, as they depend on both the quantity and the type of air fryer. In addition, cooking temperatures can be raised or lowered, and, in this case, cooking times can lengthen or shorten.

Food	Temperature C°	Time in minutes
Artichokes	180	20
Asparagus	200	10
Aubergine	200	15
Bacon	200	5
Beef eye round roast	195	45
Beef sirloin steak	200	10
Beets	200	40
Biscuits	160	15
Broccoli florets	200	10

Brussels sprouts	190	15
Burger	180	20
Carrots	190	15
Cakes	180	20
Calamari	200	4
Cauliflower florets	200	12
Chicken (whole)	200	60
Chicken breast	190	12
Chicken strips	180	10
Chicken drumstick	185	20
Chicken legs	180	20
Chicken wings	180	75
Corn on the cob	195	6
Courgettes	200	12
Cod (fillet)	200	10
Fennel	185	15
Filet mignon	200	12
Fish fillet	200	10

Flank steak	200	10	Frozen potato gems	200	20
Frozen breaded shrimp	200	10	Frozen spring rolls	195	14
Frozen cheese sticks	200	8	Green beans	200	5
Frozen chicken burger	180	10	Kale leaves	125	12
Frozen chicken nuggets	200	10	Lamb chops	200	12
Frozen crumbed prawns	200	9	Lamb roast (boneless)	180	40
Frozen fish fillets	200	14	Meatballs	190	10
Frozen fish fingers	200	10	Meatloaf	200	30
Frozen French fries	200	18	Muffins	180	15
Frozen meatballs	160	10	Mushrooms, sliced	200	5
Frozen mozzarella sticks	200	8	Mushrooms, whole	180	10
Frozen onion rings	180	10	Onion	200	10
Frozen pizza	190	10	Peppers, whole	200	12/15
			Peppers, cubed	180	10
			Pizza	180	14
			Pork chops	200	12
			Pork loin	180	20

Pork ribs	200	25
Potatoes	200	25
Pumpkin	200	10
Quiche	180	20
Rack of lamb	190	22
Rib eye	200	10
Ribs	200	15
Salmon (fillet)	190	12
Sausage	190	15
Scallops	200	5
Prawns	200	5
Sea bream	160	20
Scones	200	15
Sirloin steak	200	10
Sweet potatoes	190	30
Tuna steak	200	10
Tomatoes, whole	200	5
Tomatoes, halved	150	10
Stuffed veggies	180	10/12

RECIPES

Breakfast

Apricot muffins

PREPARATION TIME: 15 minutes I COOKING TIME: 15 minutes I SERVINGS: 12

- ✓ 300 gr of flour
- ✓ 8 apricots
- ✓ 150 gr of softened butter
- ✓ 200 gr of sugar
- ✓ 2 large eggs
- ✓ 200 ml of milk
- ✓ 6 gr of yeast
- ✓ 1 pinch of salt

DIRECTIONS

- ➤ Cut the butter into chunks and put it in a bowl.
- ➤ Add the sugar and whisk with an electric mixer until you get a creamy and thick mixture.
- ➤ Add the egg, milk, flour, yeast, and salt.
- ➤ Stir until you get a homogeneous and lump-free mixture.
- ➤ Wash the apricots, remove the stones, and then cut them into cubes.
- ➤ Place the cups inside the muffin moulds.
- ➤ Pour the mixture into the moulds and then add the apricot cubes.
- ➤ Put the moulds inside the air fryer.
- ➤ Cook at 180 ° C for 15 minutes.

- ➤ After cooking, remove the moulds from the air fryer.
- ➤ Allow to cool completely and then remove the muffins from the moulds.

Bacon and cheese omelette

PREPARATION TIME: 15 minutes I COOKING TIME: 6 minutes I SERVINGS: 4

- ✓ 6 eggs
- ✓ 4 slices of bacon
- ✓ 50 gr of grated cheddar
- ✓ Salt and pepper to taste

DIRECTIONS

- ➤ Shell the eggs in a bowl and add salt and pepper.
- ➤ Beat with a fork until you get a homogeneous mixture.
- ➤ Pour the mixture into the cake pan brushed with olive oil.
- ➤ Put the cake pan into the air fryer basket and cook at 180 ° C for 2 minutes.
- ➤ After 2 minutes, add the bacon and cheddar.
- ➤ Continue cooking for another 4 minutes.
- ➤ After cooking, remove the baking pan from the fryer.
- ➤ Divide the omelette into 4 parts, put it on plates and serve.

Basket of bacon eggs

PREPARATION TIME: 10 minutes I COOKING TIME: 15 minutes I SERVINGS: 4

- ✓ 8 slices of sandwich bread

- ✓ 4 slices of bacon
- ✓ 4 eggs
- ✓ 100 gr of cheddar
- ✓ Salt and pepper to taste

DIRECTIONS

- ➤ Take 4 cocottes and brush them with olive oil.
- ➤ Place the slices of bread inside the cocottes so that they cover them completely.
- ➤ Now put a slice of bacon in each cocotte.
- ➤ Now shell the eggs inside each cocotte and season with salt and pepper.
- ➤ Put the cocottes inside the air fryer and cook at 180 ° C for 15 minutes.
- ➤ Once cooked, remove the cocottes from the air fryer and serve immediately.

Blueberries muffins

PREPARATION TIME: 20 minutes I COOKING TIME: 15 minutes I SERVINGS: 10

- ✓ 200 gr of blueberries
- ✓ 250 gr of flour
- ✓ 50 gr of melted butter
- ✓ 250 ml of milk
- ✓ 2 medium eggs
- ✓ 80 gr of sugar
- ✓ 6 gr of instant yeast for sweets
- ✓ ½ tsp of sodium bicarbonate
- ✓ 1 pinch of salt
- ✓ Olive oil

DIRECTIONS

- ➤ Shell the egg in a bowl and add the sugar.
- ➤ Beat the eggs with an electric mixer, until you get a light and fluffy mixture.

- ➤ Put the melted butter and milk in another bowl. Mix well and then add them to the egg and sugar mixture.
- ➤ Mix well and then add the flour, yeast, sodium bicarbonate, and salt.
- ➤ Stir again until you have a lump-free mixture and finally add the blueberries.
- ➤ Mix the mixture well and then divide it into 10 muffin moulds brushed with olive oil.
- ➤ Place the moulds inside the air fryer and cook at 180 °C for 15 minutes.
- ➤ Once cooked, remove the muffins from the air fryer and let them cool.
- ➤ As soon as they have cooled, remove them from the moulds, put them on a serving dish and serve.

Cheese omelette

PREPARATION TIME: 15 minutes I COOKING TIME: 6 minutes I SERVINGS: 4

- ✓ 6 eggs
- ✓ 100 gr of cheddar
- ✓ 50 gr of Parmesan cheese
- ✓ Salt and pepper to taste

DIRECTIONS

- ➤ Shell the eggs in a bowl and add salt and pepper.
- ➤ Beat them with a fork and then add the Parmesan.
- ➤ Mix well and pour them into a baking pan brushed with olive oil.
- ➤ Put the baking pan inside the fryer and cook at 180 ° C for 2 minutes.
- ➤ After 2 minutes, add the sliced cheddar and continue cooking for another 4 minutes.

- ➤ After cooking, remove the baking pan from the fryer.
- ➤ Divide the omelette into 4 parts, put it on serving plates and serve.

Choco muffins

PREPARATION TIME: 20 minutes I COOKING TIME: 12 minutes I SERVINGS: 12

- ✓ 300 gr of flour
- ✓ 80 gr of unsweetened chocolate powder
- ✓ 280 gr of sugar
- ✓ 6 gr of instant yeast for sweets
- ✓ 4 medium eggs
- ✓ 200 ml of milk
- ✓ 150 gr of softened butter
- ✓ 1 pinch of sodium bicarbonate

DIRECTIONS

- ➤ Put the flour, sugar, instant yeast, sodium bicarbonate and coconut flour in a bowl. Mix everything well.
- ➤ Cut the butter into chunks and put it in a bowl.
- ➤ Add the egg and whisk with an electric mixer until you get a puffy and frothy mixture.
- ➤ Add the milk and continue mixing.
- ➤ Now add the flour mix and mix until you get a lump-free mixture.
- ➤ Place the cups inside the muffin moulds.
- ➤ Put the mixture inside the cups.
- ➤ Put the moulds inside the air fryer and cook at 180 °C for 12 minutes.
- ➤ After cooking, remove the moulds from the air fryer.
- ➤ Allow to cool completely, then remove the muffins from the moulds and serve.

Crumpets

PREPARATION TIME: 20 minutes I COOKING TIME: 24 minutes I SERVINGS: 6

- ✓ 100 gr of flour 0
- ✓ 100 ml of milk
- ✓ 50 ml of warm water
- ✓ 5 grams of sugar
- ✓ 2 gr of dry yeast
- ✓ A pinch gr of salt
- ✓ 1 gr of baking soda

DIRECTIONS

- ➤ Melt the yeast and sugar with the milk in a bowl.
- ➤ Mix well and then add the sifted flour.
- ➤ Continue to mix with a whisk until you get a homogeneous mixture without lumps.
- ➤ Dissolve the baking soda in 20 ml of water and then add it to the mixture.
- ➤ Stir until you get a thick batter.
- ➤ Put the mixture to rest for 10 minutes.
- ➤ Put a sheet of parchment paper cut out of the same size as the basket of the air fryer and put a little mixture inside.
- ➤ Close the fryer and cook at 200 ° C, two minutes per side.
- ➤ Proceed in the same way until the end of the batter.
- ➤ Once the crumpets are cooked, put them on serving plates and serve.

Double cheese toast

PREPARATION TIME: 10 minutes I COOKING TIME: 4 minutes I SERVINGS: 4

- ✓ 12 slices of toast bread
- ✓ 8 slices of cheddar

✓ 8 slices of Emmental

DIRECTIONS

- Put two slices of cheddar and two slices of Emmental on 4 slices of bread.
- Place 4 more slices of bread on top and repeat the operation.
- Close with the last 4 slices of bread and place the toast inside the air fryer.
- Cook at 180 ° C, 2 minutes per side.
- Once cooked, remove the toast from the fryer and place them on serving plates.
- Divide the toast in half and serve.

English muffins

PREPARATION TIME: 20 minutes I REST TIME: 1 hour and 30 minutes I COOKING TIME: 10 minutes I SERVINGS: 10

- ✓ 300 gr of flour
- ✓ 50 gr of sugar
- ✓ 100 ml of water
- ✓ 1 tsp of instant yeast
- ✓ 200 ml of whole milk
- ✓ 2 large eggs
- ✓ 60 gr of melted butter
- ✓ ½ tsp of salt

DIRECTIONS

- Put the water, milk, and sugar in a glass jug. Stir and heat in the microwave for 40 seconds.
- Now add the yeast and stir until it is completely incorporated.
- Let it sit for 8 minutes or until the yeast becomes foamy.
- At this point, add the butter and egg and mix again.
- Put the flour and salt in a bowl and then pour the liquid mixture.

- Pour the liquid mixture slowly and without ever stopping mixing, until you get a smooth and lump-free mixture.
- Transfer the mixture to a bowl brushed with olive oil and cover with cling film.
- Let the dough rise for 60 minutes.
- After the hour, roll out the dough on a floured surface until you obtain a pastry with a thickness of about 1 centimetre.
- With a pastry cutter, make some slices of the dough.
- Put the muffins in the pan, cover them with a kitchen towel and let them rise for another 30 minutes.
- After 30 minutes, put the muffins inside the air fryer.
- Cook at 180 ° C, 5 minutes per side.
- Once cooked, remove the muffins from the air fryer.
- Let them cool, then put them on serving plates and serve.

Ham and cheese toast

PREPARATION TIME: 10 minutes I COOKING TIME: 4 minutes I SERVINGS: 4

- ✓ 8 slices of sandwich bread
- ✓ 8 slices of cooked ham
- ✓ 8 slices of cheddar

DIRECTIONS

- Take 4 slices of bread and put two slices of ham and two of cheddar on top.
- Close with the other half of the bread and place the toast inside the air fryer.
- Bake at 180 ° C for 4 minutes, turning the toasts halfway through cooking.
- Once cooked, remove the toast from the air fryer.

- ➤ Put the toasts on the plates, divide them in half and serve.

Lemon and yogurt muffins

PREPARATION TIME: 20 minutes I COOKING TIME: 12 minutes I SERVINGS: 10

- ✓ 300 gr of flour
- ✓ 4 eggs
- ✓ 150 gr of sugar
- ✓ 60 gr of melted butter
- ✓ 125 gr of yogurt
- ✓ 6 gr of instant yeast for sweets
- ✓ ½ lemon

DIRECTIONS

- ➤ Wash and dry the lemon, grate the zest, and strain the juice into a bowl.
- ➤ Put the eggs, lemon juice and melted butter in a bowl.
- ➤ Mix until the mixture is light and fluffy.
- ➤ Put the flour, baking powder, lemon zest and sugar in another bowl and mix well.
- ➤ Pour the flour mixture into the bowl with the eggs and mix until you get a smooth and lump-free mixture.
- ➤ Place the cups inside the muffin moulds.
- ➤ Pour the mixture into the cups.
- ➤ Place the moulds inside the air fryer and cook at 180 ° C for 12 minutes.
- ➤ After cooking, remove the moulds from the air fryer and allow to cool completely.
- ➤ Remove the muffins from the moulds, sprinkle them with icing sugar and serve.

Omelette with courgettes and cheese

PREPARATION TIME: 20 minutes I COOKING TIME: 11 minutes I SERVINGS 4

- ✓ 8 eggs
- ✓ 4 small courgettes
- ✓ 2 shallots
- ✓ 6 slices of cheddar
- ✓ 1 sprig of chopped basil
- ✓ Olive oil to taste
- ✓ Salt and pepper to taste

DIRECTIONS

- ➤ Check the courgettes, wash them, and then cut them into small pieces.
- ➤ Put the courgettes in the basket of the air fryer and season with oil, salt, and pepper.
- ➤ Cook at 180 ° C for 5 minutes, then remove them and put them in a bowl.
- ➤ Peel the shallots, then chop them and place them in the bowl with the courgettes.
- ➤ Shell the eggs in another bowl and add salt and pepper.
- ➤ Beat them well with a fork and then pour them into the bowl with the courgettes.
- ➤ Pour the mixture into the cake pan brushed with olive oil.
- ➤ Put the cake pan in the air fryer and cook at 180 ° C for 2 minutes.
- ➤ After 2 minutes, add the basil and cheddar and continue cooking for another 4 minutes.
- ➤ After cooking, remove the baking pan from the air fryer.
- ➤ Cut the omelette into 4 parts, put it on serving plates and serve.

Scones

PREPARATION TIME: 25 minutes I REST TIME: 20 minutes I COOKING TIME: 12 minutes I SERVINGS: 8

- ✓ 100 grams of flour
- ✓ 75 ml of milk
- ✓ 25 gr of butter softened at room temperature
- ✓ 5 grams of sugar
- ✓ 1 gr of salt

DIRECTIONS

- ➢ Arrange the flour on a pastry board.
- ➢ Add salt, yeast and sugar and give the flour the typical fountain shape.
- ➢ Cut the butter into chunks and add it to the flour.
- ➢ Put the milk in the centre of the flour and start kneading with your hands.
- ➢ Knead until the mixture is compact and a little sticky.
- ➢ Form the mixture into a loaf, wrap it in cling film and refrigerate for 20 minutes.
- ➢ After 20 minutes, take the dough and roll it out with a rolling pin to form a sheet of 1.5 cm.
- ➢ Now make discs of 6.5 cm each.
- ➢ Put the dough discs inside the air fryer.
- ➢ Beat an egg with a little milk and then brush the surface of the dough discs.
- ➢ Cook at 200 ° C for 12 minutes.
- ➢ Once cooked, remove the scones from the air fryer and let them cool.
- ➢ When they have cooled, put them on serving plates and serve with jam to taste.

Toast with avocado and egg

PREPARATION TIME: 15 minutes I COOKING TIME: 4 minutes I SERVINGS 4

- ✓ 8 slices of toast bread
- ✓ 3 small avocados
- ✓ 1 lime
- ✓ 4 hard-boiled eggs
- ✓ Olive oil to taste
- ✓ Salt and pepper to taste

DIRECTIONS

- ➢ Brush the slices of bread with olive oil and place them inside the air fryer.
- ➢ Bake at 180 ° C, two minutes per side, then remove the bread from the fryer and place it on a plate.
- ➢ Meanwhile, shell the eggs and cut them into slices.
- ➢ Peel the avocados, remove the stones, and put the pulp in a bowl.
- ➢ Mash the avocado pulp with a fork and then add the lime juice, salt and pepper and mix well.
- ➢ Spread the avocado pulp over 4 slices of bread and then add the egg slices.
- ➢ Cover with the other 4 slices of bread and serve.

Yorkshire pudding

PREPARATION TIME: 20 minutes I REST TIME: 30 minutes I COOKING TIME: 20 minutes I SERVINGS: 4

- ✓ 100 gr of flour
- ✓ 2 medium eggs
- ✓ 100 ml of milk
- ✓ Seed oil to taste

✓ Salt and pepper to taste

DIRECTIONS

➢ Shell the eggs in a bowl and add the flour.
➢ Mix with an electric mixer until you get a smooth and homogeneous mixture.
➢ Add the milk slowly and continue to mix until you get a homogeneous mixture.
➢ Put the mixture in the fridge and let it rest for 30 minutes.
➢ After 30 minutes, take the mixture from the fridge.
➢ Brush the muffin moulds with olive oil and place them inside the air fryer.
➢ Heat them to 200 ° C for 5 minutes.
➢ Remove the moulds and divide the mixture, filling them up to ¾.
➢ Put the moulds back inside the air fryer and cook at 200 ° C for 20 minutes.
➢ After cooking, remove the moulds from the fryer.
➢ Serve the Yorkshire puddings immediately by taking them out of the moulds very gently to prevent them from breaking.

Poultry

Chicken breast with corn flakes breading

PREPARATION TIME: 15 minutes I COOKING TIME: 14 minutes I SERVINGS: 4

✓ 4 chicken breast
✓ 10 ml of milk
✓ 100 gr of corn flakes
✓ 2 eggs
✓ Salt and pepper to taste
✓ Olive oil to taste

DIRECTIONS

➢ Put the corn flakes in the mixer and chop them finely and put them on a plate.
➢ Wash and pat the chicken with a paper towel and then cut it into thin slices.
➢ Put the milk and eggs in a bowl, add salt and pepper and mix well with a fork.
➢ Pass the chicken slices first in the egg and then in the corn flakes.
➢ Brush the basket of the air fryer with olive oil and put the chicken inside.
➢ Sprinkle a little oil on the surface and cook for 7 minutes per side at 200 ° C.
➢ Once cooked, take the chicken out of the fryer, put it on plates and serve.

Sweet Chicken

PREPARATION TIME: 20 minutes I COOKING TIME: 16 minutes I SERVINGS: 4

✓ 500 gr of chicken breasts
✓ 2 spring onions
✓ 3 shallots

- ✓ 2 pears
- ✓ 1 glass of cider
- ✓ 1 tbsp of honey
- ✓ Salt and pepper to taste

DIRECTIONS

- ➢ Wash and pat the chicken breasts with a paper towel and then divide them into 4 parts.
- ➢ Brush the baking pan with olive oil and put the chicken breasts inside.
- ➢ Peel the shallots and then cut them into thin slices.
- ➢ Clean the spring onions and then cut them into rings.
- ➢ Peel the pears, remove the seeds and the core, and then cut them into slices.
- ➢ Put the spring onions, shallots, and pears in the baking pan with the chicken.
- ➢ Season with salt and pepper and then sprinkle with the cider and honey.
- ➢ Put the baking pan inside the air fryer.
- ➢ Cook at 200 ° C for 16 minutes, turning the chicken halfway through cooking.
- ➢ After cooking, remove the baking pan from the air fryer.
- ➢ Put the chicken, pears, spring onions and shallots on the plates, sprinkle with the cooking juices and serve.

Chicken drumsticks with bacon and green olives

PREPARATION TIME: 15 minutes I COOKING TIME: 30 minutes I SERVINGS: 4

- ✓ 4 chicken drumsticks of 250 gr each
- ✓ 8 slices of bacon
- ✓ 150 gr of green olives
- ✓ 1 onion

- ✓ 1 glass of white wine
- ✓ 1 lemon
- ✓ 3 sprigs of rosemary
- ✓ Salt and pepper to taste
- ✓ Olive oil to taste

DIRECTIONS

- ➢ Wash and pat the chicken drumsticks with a paper towel and then roll them up with the bacon.
- ➢ Brush a baking pan with olive oil and put the melts inside.
- ➢ Wash and dry the rosemary and place it in the pan.
- ➢ Season with oil, salt and pepper and put the baking pan inside the air fryer.
- ➢ Cook at 180 ° C for 5 minutes.
- ➢ After 5 minutes, blend with the wine, sprinkle with lemon juice and add the olives.
- ➢ Continue cooking at 180 ° C for another 25 minutes.
- ➢ After cooking, remove the baking pan from the air fryer.
- ➢ Put the chicken drumsticks and the olives on the plates and serve.

Chicken legs with mushrooms, potatoes, and peas

PREPARATION TIME: 20 minutes I COOKING TIME: 30 minutes I SERVINGS: 4

- ✓ 4 chicken legs of 250 gr each
- ✓ 200 gr of already shelled fresh peas
- ✓ 200 gr of champignon mushrooms
- ✓ 4 small potatoes
- ✓ 2 sprigs of chopped thyme
- ✓ 1 onion

- ✓ Salt and pepper to taste
- ✓ Olive oil to taste

DIRECTIONS

- ➢ Peel and wash the potatoes, cut them into cubes and place them in a baking pan brushed with olive oil.
- ➢ Rinse the peas and put them in the baking pan.
- ➢ Remove the earthy part of the mushrooms. Wash them, dry them well and then cut them into slices.
- ➢ Peel the onion and then chop it.
- ➢ Wash and pat the chicken with a paper towel.
- ➢ Put the chicken and mushrooms in the baking pan with the potatoes.
- ➢ Season everything with oil, salt and pepper and sprinkle with thyme.
- ➢ Put the baking pan inside the air fryer and cook at 180 ° C for 30 minutes.
- ➢ After cooking, remove the baking pan from the air fryer.
- ➢ Place the chicken, potatoes, mushrooms, and peas on the plate and serve.

Chicken, mushrooms, and cherry tomatoes

PREPARATION TIME: 20 minutes I COOKING TIME: 30 minutes I SERVINGS: 4

- ✓ 600 gr of chicken drumsticks
- ✓ 300 gr of champignon mushrooms
- ✓ 12 cherry tomatoes
- ✓ 1 glass of white wine
- ✓ 1 clove of garlic
- ✓ 1 tbsp of chopped parsley
- ✓ Salt and pepper to taste
- ✓ Olive oil to taste

DIRECTIONS

- ➢ Peel the garlic and then chop it.
- ➢ Remove the final part of the stem from the mushrooms, then wash them, dry them, and cut them into slices.
- ➢ Wash the cherry tomatoes and then cut them in half.
- ➢ Brush a baking pan with olive oil and put the chicken drumsticks inside.
- ➢ Add the cherry tomatoes and mushrooms.
- ➢ Sprinkle with garlic and parsley and season with oil, salt, and pepper.
- ➢ Sprinkle with white wine and place the baking pan inside the air fryer.
- ➢ Cook at 180°C for 30 minutes, turning the meat every 10 minutes.
- ➢ After cooking, remove the baking pan from the air fryer.
- ➢ Put the chicken, the cherry tomatoes and the mushrooms on the serving plates and serve.

Chicken Nuggets

PREPARATION TIME: 20 minutes I REST TIME: 1 hour in the fridge I COOKING TIME: 10 minutes I SERVINGS: 4

- ✓ 600 gr of ground chicken
- ✓ 1 tsp of minced garlic
- ✓ 1 tsp of chopped onion
- ✓ 150 grams of flour
- ✓ 150 of corn starch
- ✓ 2 eggs
- ✓ 500 ml of milk
- ✓ 500 ml of iced sparkling water
- ✓ Salt and pepper to taste
- ✓ Olive oil to taste

DIRECTIONS

- ➤ Put the chicken meat in a bowl and add salt, pepper, garlic, and onion.
- ➤ Stir until you get a homogeneous mixture.
- ➤ Now form balls, mash them, and arrange them on a tray covered with parchment paper. Leave to rest for 1 hour in the refrigerator.
- ➤ Now put 100 g of flour and 100 g of corn starch and the sparkling water in a bowl and the eggs and milk in another.
- ➤ Mix the flour mix well until you get a homogeneous and lump-free mixture.
- ➤ Do the same with the eggs and milk.
- ➤ Put the rest of the flour and corn starch on a plate.
- ➤ Take the chicken and pass it first in the batter, then in the eggs and finally in the flour.
- ➤ Place the nuggets in the basket of the air fryer and sprinkle some oil on the surface.
- ➤ Close the basket and cook at 200 ° C for 10 minutes, 5 minutes per side.
- ➤ Once cooked, remove the nuggets from the fryer, place them on plates and serve.

Chicken with garlic, thyme, and rosemary

PREPARATION TIME: 20 minutes I COOKING TIME: 15 minutes I SERVINGS: 4

- ✓ 800 gr of chicken breast
- ✓ 2 limes
- ✓ 1 clove of garlic
- ✓ 3 sprigs of thyme
- ✓ 3 sprigs of rosemary
- ✓ The grated rind of an orange
- ✓ Olive oil to taste
- ✓ Salt and pepper to taste

DIRECTIONS

- ➤ Peel and chop the garlic clove.
- ➤ Wash and chop the sprigs of thyme and rosemary as well.
- ➤ Mix the minced garlic with the olive oil, thyme, rosemary, and orange zest.
- ➤ Remove the excess fat from the chicken breast, wash it and pat it dry with a paper towel.
- ➤ Wash and dry the limes and then cut them into slices.
- ➤ Divide the chicken in half horizontally and place the lime slices inside.
- ➤ Brush the chicken with the garlic and herb mixture.
- ➤ Put the chicken inside the fryer and cook at 200 ° C for 15 minutes, turning the meat halfway through cooking.
- ➤ When the chicken is cooked, take it out of the air fryer and place it on a cutting board.
- ➤ Cut the chicken into slices, put it on serving plates and serve.

Chicken with laurel

PREPARATION TIME: 20 minutes I COOKING TIME: 30 minutes I SERVINGS: 4

- ✓ 1 whole 800 gr chicken cut into pieces
- ✓ 1 red onion
- ✓ 1 glass of white wine
- ✓ 4 bay leaves
- ✓ 1 cup of chicken broth
- ✓ Flour to taste
- ✓ Salt and pepper to taste
- ✓ Olive oil to taste

DIRECTIONS

➤ Peel the onion and cut it into thin slices.
➤ Wash the chicken and pat it dry with a paper towel.
➤ Wash and dry the bay leaf.
➤ Brush the chicken with olive oil and then pass it in the flour, flour it well on all sides.
➤ Brush a baking pan with olive oil and put the chicken and bay leaf inside.
➤ Add the onion, season with salt and pepper and sprinkle with white wine.
➤ Put the baking pan in the air fryer and cook at 180 ° C for 5 minutes.
➤ After 5 minutes, sprinkle with the chicken broth and continue cooking for another 30 minutes, turning the meat from time to time.
➤ After cooking, remove the baking pan from the air fryer.
➤ Put the chicken on serving plates.
➤ Blend the cooking juices with an immersion blender, sprinkle the chicken and serve.

Chicken with leeks

PREPARATION TIME: 20 minutes I COOKING TIME: 30 minutes I SERVINGS: 4

✓ 800 gr of whole chicken cut into pieces
✓ 5 leeks
✓ 1 clove of garlic
✓ ½ glass of white wine
✓ 50 gr of flour
✓ Olive oil to taste
✓ Salt and pepper to taste

DIRECTIONS

➤ Wash the chicken, pat it dry with a paper towel and brush it with a little oil.
➤ Dip the chicken pieces in flour and flour well on all sides.
➤ Wash the leeks and then cut them into rings.
➤ Put the leeks and chicken in a baking pan.
➤ Peel the garlic and then chop it.
➤ Season with oil, salt and pepper and sprinkle with garlic and white wine.
➤ Put the baking pan in the air fryer and cook at 200 °C for 30 minutes, turning the meat every 10 minutes.
➤ After cooking, remove the baking pan from the air fryer.
➤ Put the chicken and leeks on plates, sprinkle with the cooking juices and serve.

Chicken with pumpkin

PREPARATION TIME: 20 minutes I COOKING TIME: 30 minutes I SERVINGS: 4

✓ 800 gr of chicken legs
✓ 400 gr of pumpkin pulp
✓ 1 onion
✓ 1 pomegranate
✓ 1 clove of garlic
✓ 6 sprigs of thyme
✓ Salt and pepper to taste
✓ Olive oil to taste

DIRECTIONS

➤ Wash and dry the pumpkin pulp and cut it into cubes.
➤ Wash and dry the chicken legs.
➤ Peel and chop the garlic.
➤ Shell the pomegranate and collect the grains in a bowl.
➤ Wash and dry the thyme.

- ➤ Put the pumpkin and chicken in a bowl brushed with olive oil.
- ➤ Add the thyme, season with oil, salt and pepper and sprinkle with minced garlic.
- ➤ Place the chicken in the fryer and cook at 190 °C for 30 minutes, turning the meat halfway through cooking.
- ➤ After cooking, remove the baking pan from the air fryer.
- ➤ Put the chicken and pumpkin on the serving plates, sprinkle with the pomegranate grains and serve.

Curry marinated chicken with apples

PREPARATION TIME: 20 minutes I REST TIME: 40 minutes I COOKING TIME: 15 minutes I SERVINGS: 4

- ✓ 800 gr of chicken breast
- ✓ 4 apples
- ✓ 30 gr of butter
- ✓ 1 tbsp of curry powder
- ✓ 1 onion
- ✓ 1 lemon
- ✓ 260 grams of Greek yogurt
- ✓ 2 tbsp of chopped parsley
- ✓ 2 tsp of brown sugar
- ✓ Salt and pepper to taste
- ✓ Olive oil to taste

DIRECTIONS

- ➤ Wash the chicken breast, pat it dry with a paper towel and then cut it in half.
- ➤ Remove the excess fat and then put it in a bowl.
- ➤ Peel the onion, chop it, and place it in the bowl with the chicken.

- ➤ Add the yogurt, curry, salt, and pepper and mix well.
- ➤ Put the bowl in the fridge and marinate for 40 minutes.
- ➤ Meanwhile, peel the apples, remove the seeds and core, cut them into wedges and place them in a bowl.
- ➤ Sprinkle them with lemon juice and set aside.
- ➤ After 40 minutes, take the chicken from the fridge, drain it, and then put it inside the air fryer.
- ➤ Cook at 180 ° C for 15 minutes, turning the chicken halfway through cooking.
- ➤ While the chicken is cooking, melt the butter in a saucepan.
- ➤ When the butter has melted, add the apples, sugar, salt, and pepper, and cook for 5 minutes, stirring often.
- ➤ Once cooked, remove the chicken from the air fryer.
- ➤ Put it on a cutting board, cut it into slices and place on serving plates.
- ➤ Add the apples with the cooking juices and serve.

Chicken with black olives

PREPARATION TIME: 20 minutes I COOKING TIME: 30 minutes I SERVINGS: 4

- ✓ 800g of chicken breast, cut into pieces
- ✓ 4 sage leaves
- ✓ 2 sprigs of marjoram
- ✓ 2 sprigs of thyme
- ✓ 100 gr of black olives, halved
- ✓ 1 minced garlic
- ✓ Salt and pepper to taste
- ✓ Olive oil to taste

DIRECTIONS

- ➤ Wash and dry marjoram, sage, and thyme.
- ➤ Place the chicken breast in the air fryer.
- ➤ Add sage, marjoram, and thyme.
- ➤ Sprinkle with chopped garlic and season with oil, salt, and pepper.
- ➤ Add the olives and close the fryer.
- ➤ Cook at 180 ° C for 30 minutes.
- ➤ Check the cooking and, if the meat is not cooked yet, continue for another 5 minutes.

Fried chicken wings with vinegar sauce

PREPARATION TIME: 20 minutes I COOKING TIME: 20 minutes I SERVINGS: 4

- ✓ 12 chicken wings
- ✓ 8 tbsp of flour
- ✓ 2 cloves of garlic
- ✓ 4 tbsp of white wine vinegar
- ✓ Chopped parsley to taste
- ✓ Salt and pepper to taste
- ✓ Olive oil to taste

DIRECTIONS

- ➤ Cut the chicken wings in half, remove the bony tip, then wash and blot with absorbent paper.
- ➤ Put the flour on a plate.
- ➤ Brush the chicken wings with olive oil, season with salt and pepper and then flour them well on both sides.
- ➤ Brush the basket of the air fryer with olive oil and place the chicken wings inside.
- ➤ Sprinkle a little oil on the surface, close the basket and cook at 200 ° C for 20 minutes, turning the wings halfway through cooking.

- ➤ Meanwhile, prepare the vinegar sauce.
- ➤ Peel the garlic cloves and place them in the blender glass.
- ➤ Add salt, pepper, parsley, vinegar, and oil.
- ➤ Blend until you get a smooth and homogeneous sauce.
- ➤ Once cooked, remove the chicken wings from the air fryer.
- ➤ Put the wings on plates, sprinkle them with the vinegar sauce and serve.

Fried chicken with ginger

PREPARATION TIME: 20 minutes I COOKING TIME: 15 minutes I SERVINGS: 4

- ✓ 400 gr of chicken breast
- ✓ Fresh grated ginger to taste
- ✓ 100 ml of white wine
- ✓ 100 ml of soy sauce
- ✓ Corn flour to taste
- ✓ Flour to taste
- ✓ Salt and pepper to taste
- ✓ Olive oil to taste

DIRECTIONS

- ➤ Remove the excess fat from the chicken and then cut it into cubes.
- ➤ Put the chicken in a bowl and season with the ginger, salt, pepper, wine, oil and soy sauce.
- ➤ Mix well, cover the bowl, refrigerate, and marinate for 30 minutes.
- ➤ After 30 minutes, put the cornmeal and flour on a plate and mix well.
- ➤ Flour the chicken cubes in the flour mix and place them in the basket of the air fryer.
- ➤ Sprinkle a little oil on the surface and cook at 180 ° C for 15 minutes, turning the chicken halfway through cooking.

- Once cooked, take the chicken out of the air fryer, put it on plates and serve.

Guinea fowl with grapes

PREPARATION TIME: 25 minutes I COOKING TIME: 25 minutes I SERVINGS: 4

- ✓ 1 guinea fowl of 1.2 kg cut into pieces
- ✓ 2 bunches of white grapes
- ✓ 3 sage leaves
- ✓ 4 juniper berries
- ✓ ½ glass of white wine
- ✓ ½ glass of brandy
- ✓ Olive oil to taste
- ✓ Salt and pepper to taste

DIRECTIONS

- Wash the sage leaves and then chop them.
- Put the guinea fowl in a baking pan brushed with olive oil.
- Wash the berries, cut them in half and remove the seeds.
- Put the grapes in the baking pan with the guinea fowl.
- Season with oil, salt, and pepper.
- Sprinkle with sage, juniper, wine, and brandy and place the baking pan inside the air fryer.
- Cook at 180 ° C for 25 minutes, turning the meat after 10 minutes.
- After cooking, remove the baking pan from the air fryer.
- Put the guinea fowl and grapes on the plates, sprinkle with the cooking juices and serve.

Chicken with orange

PREPARATION TIME: 15 minutes I COOKING TIME: 20 minutes I SERVINGS: 4

- ✓ chicken breast of 800 gr cut into pieces
- ✓ 2 oranges
- ✓ 1 clove of garlic
- ✓ 2 sprigs of thyme
- ✓ 4 sage leaves
- ✓ 1 glass of Cointreau
- ✓ Salt and pepper to taste
- ✓ Olive oil to taste

DIRECTIONS

- Put the chicken breast in a baking pan brushed with olive oil.
- Peel the garlic, chop it, and sprinkle it over the guinea fowl.
- Wash the sage and thyme and put them in the baking pan.
- Season everything with oil, salt and pepper and put the baking pan inside the fryer.
- Cook at 180 ° C for 5 minutes.
- After 5 minutes, sprinkle with the Cointreau and the squeezed orange juice.
- Continue cooking for another 15 minutes.
- After cooking, remove the baking pan from the air fryer.
- Put the guinea fowl on the plates, sprinkle with the cooking juices and serve.

Herb turkey burger

PREPARATION TIME: 20 minutes I COOKING TIME: 10 minutes I SERVINGS: 4

- ✓ 600 gr of minced turkey breast

- ✓ 1 tbsp of chopped thyme
- ✓ 1 tbsp of chopped rosemary
- ✓ 2 chopped sage leaves
- ✓ 1 tbsp of mustard
- ✓ Ketchup to taste
- ✓ Mayonnaise to taste
- ✓ Salt and pepper to taste
- ✓ Salt and pepper to taste

DIRECTIONS

- ➢ Put the meat in a bowl. Add the chopped herbs, salt, pepper, and mustard.
- ➢ Mix first with a fork and then knead the mixture with your hands.
- ➢ Take half of the mixture and form a meatball which you will then lightly crush with your hands.
- ➢ Do the same with the other half of the mixture.
- ➢ Put the burgers inside the air fryer.
- ➢ Cook at 180 ° C, 5 minutes per side.
- ➢ Once cooked, remove the burgers from the air fryer.
- ➢ Put the burgers on serving plates, toss with ketchup and mayonnaise and serve.

Mint chicken breast with yogurt sauce

PREPARATION TIME: 25 minutes I REST TIME: 1 hour I COOKING TIME: 16 minutes I SERVINGS: 4

- ✓ 600 gr of chicken breast
- ✓ 2 cucumbers
- ✓ 120 gr of Greek yogurt
- ✓ 1 green apple
- ✓ 1 small pineapple
- ✓ 1 lemon
- ✓ 12 fresh mint leaves

- ✓ 1 bay leaf
- ✓ Olive oil to taste
- ✓ Salt and pepper to taste

DIRECTIONS

- ➢ Wash and pat the chicken breast with a paper towel and then cut it in half.
- ➢ Put it in a bowl and season with oil, salt, pepper, lemon juice.
- ➢ Mix well and then add the bay leaf.
- ➢ Cover the bowl with cling film, refrigerate and marinate for 1 hour.
- ➢ After the hour, take the chicken out of the fridge and put it inside the air fryer.
- ➢ Wash and dry the mint leaves, chop them, and sprinkle them on the chicken.
- ➢ Cook at 180 ° C for 8 minutes per side.
- ➢ Meanwhile, wash the apple without peeling it, remove the seeds and core and then cut it into thin slices.
- ➢ Take the pineapple pulp, wash it, and then cut it into cubes.
- ➢ Peel the cucumbers, wash them, and cut them into thin slices.
- ➢ Put the cucumbers, pineapple and apple in a bowl and season with oil, salt and pepper and the Greek yogurt.
- ➢ Once cooked, remove the chicken from the air fryer and place it on a cutting board.
- ➢ Cut the chicken into thin slices and place them on plates.
- ➢ Add the apple, cucumbers and pineapple and serve.

Roast turkey with pomegranate

PREPARATION TIME: 20 minutes I REST TIME: 1 hour I COOKING TIME: 40 minutes I SERVINGS: 4

- ✓ 600 gr of turkey breast
- ✓ 1 clove of garlic
- ✓ 1 pomegranate
- ✓ 75 gr of bacon
- ✓ 1 sprig of sage
- ✓ 1 sprig of thyme
- ✓ 1 sprig of rosemary
- ✓ 2 bay leaves
- ✓ Salt and pepper to taste
- ✓ Olive oil to taste

DIRECTIONS

- ➤ Shell the pomegranate and crush the grains to extract the juice.
- ➤ Remove the excess turkey fat and then put it in a bowl.
- ➤ Sprinkle with pomegranate juice, oil, salt, and pepper and marinate for 1 hour.
- ➤ Meanwhile, peel the garlic and then chop it.
- ➤ Wash thyme, sage, bay leaf and rosemary and then chop them.
- ➤ After the hour, put the bacon on a work surface one slice next to the other and sprinkle the chopped herbs and garlic on top.
- ➤ Drain the turkey and place it on top of the bacon slices.
- ➤ Roll the bacon around the turkey.
- ➤ Tie with kitchen twine and place inside the air fryer.
- ➤ Cook at 170 ° C for 40 minutes, turning every 10 minutes.
- ➤ Once cooked, remove the turkey from the fryer and place it on a cutting board.
- ➤ Remove the string and then cut the meat into slices.
- ➤ Put the meat on serving plates and serve.

Oriental fried chicken

PREPARATION TIME: 15 minutes I REST TIME: 30 MINUTES I COOKING TIME: 15 minutes I SERVINGS: 4

- ✓ 800 gr of chicken breast
- ✓ 40 ml of sesame seed oil
- ✓ 40 ml of soy sauce
- ✓ 40 ml of sake
- ✓ Mixed roasted sesame seeds to taste
- ✓ Flour to taste
- ✓ Salt and pepper to taste
- ✓ Olive oil to taste

DIRECTIONS

- ➤ Wash and dry the chicken and cut it into cubes.
- ➤ Put the chicken in a bowl and add the seed oil, soy sauce, salt, pepper and the sake.
- ➤ Mix well and marinate for 30 minutes.
- ➤ After 30 minutes, add plenty of flour in a bowl and put the chicken inside.
- ➤ Stir until all the cubes are well floured.
- ➤ Brush the basket of the air fryer with olive oil and put the chicken inside.
- ➤ Sprinkle with olive oil and cook at 200 ° C for 15 minutes, stirring the meat every 5 minutes.
- ➤ Once cooked, take the chicken out of the air fryer, and place it on the plates.
- ➤ Sprinkle with sesame seeds and serve.

Roast turkey with potatoes and onions

PREPARATION TIME: 20 minutes I COOKING TIME: 25 minutes I SERVINGS: 4

- ✓ 800 gr of turkey breast
- ✓ 2 potatoes
- ✓ 2 onions
- ✓ 1 clove of garlic
- ✓ 2 glasses of beer
- ✓ Salt and pepper to taste
- ✓ Olive oil to taste

DIRECTIONS

- ➢ Eliminate the excess fat from the turkey breast.
- ➢ Peel and wash the potatoes and then cut into cubes.
- ➢ Peel the onions and then cut into thin slices.
- ➢ Peel the garlic and then chop it.
- ➢ Put the onions and potatoes in a baking pan brushed with olive oil.
- ➢ Place the turkey breast on top.
- ➢ Sprinkle with chopped garlic and season with oil, salt and pepper and then sprinkle with beer.
- ➢ Put the baking pan inside the air fryer and cook at 200 ° C for 25 minutes.
- ➢ After cooking, remove the baking pan from the fryer.
- ➢ Place the turkey on a cutting board and cut it into slices.
- ➢ Place the turkey slices on the plates, add the onions and potatoes and serve.

Stuffed turkey breast

PREPARATION TIME: 20 minutes I COOKING TIME: 50 minutes I SERVINGS: 4

- ✓ 800 gr of turkey breast
- ✓ 2 sprigs of thyme
- ✓ 2 sprigs of rosemary
- ✓ 150 gr of cheddar
- ✓ 3 carrots
- ✓ 3 courgettes
- ✓ 100 gr of spinach
- ✓ 100 gr of cooked ham
- ✓ 200 ml of vegetable broth
- ✓ Salt and pepper to taste
- ✓ Olive oil to taste

DIRECTIONS

- ➢ Place the turkey on a cutting board, divide it in half horizontally and tap it lightly to flatten it.
- ➢ Wash and dry the thyme and rosemary and chop them.
- ➢ Peel and wash the carrots and then cut them into thin slices.
- ➢ Check and wash the courgettes and cut them into slices.
- ➢ Wash and dry the spinach.
- ➢ Season the turkey with salt and pepper and then put the chopped thyme and rosemary on the surface.
- ➢ Now add the courgettes, carrots, spinach, ham and finally the sliced cheddar.
- ➢ Begin to roll the turkey breast on itself, being careful to keep the filling an inch from the edge so that it does not come out during cooking.
- ➢ Tie the meat with string making several turns along the length, firmly locking the

ends of the thread at the ends of the shorter sides.

- ➢ Brush the turkey with olive oil and place it inside a baking pan.
- ➢ Sprinkle the turkey with the vegetable broth.
- ➢ Put the baking pan inside the air fryer and cook at 180 ° C for 50 minutes.
- ➢ Turn the turkey every 10 minutes and wet it with the cooking juices.
- ➢ After cooking, remove the baking pan from the air fryer.
- ➢ Place the turkey on a cutting board and remove the kitchen string.
- ➢ Cut the turkey into slices, put it on plates, sprinkle with the cooking juices and serve.

Stuffed turkey breast with cheese, nuts, and pepper

PREPARATION TIME: 20 minutes I COOKING TIME: 40 minutes I SERVINGS: 4

- ✓ 800 gr of turkey breast
- ✓ 50 gr of Emmental
- ✓ 40 gr of walnut kernels
- ✓ 1 sprig of rosemary
- ✓ 80 gr of sliced bacon
- ✓ Salt and pepper to taste
- ✓ Olive oil to taste

DIRECTIONS

- ➢ Wash and dry the rosemary and put it in the mixer.
- ➢ Add the walnuts, diced cheese, salt and pepper.
- ➢ Run the mixer and chop everything finely.

- ➢ Cut the turkey breast in half and flatten it with a meat mallet.
- ➢ Place the bacon on a sheet of parchment paper and place the turkey on top.
- ➢ Sprinkle the filling on the surface of the turkey.
- ➢ Roll up the turkey and bacon with the help of parchment paper.
- ➢ Tie the meat with string making several turns along the length, firmly locking the ends of the thread at the ends of the shorter sides.
- ➢ Put the turkey inside the air fryer.
- ➢ Wash the rosemary and put it in the deep fryer with the turkey.
- ➢ Close the fryer and cook at 200 ° for 40 minutes, turning the meat every 10 minutes.
- ➢ Once cooked, remove the turkey from the air fryer and place it on a cutting board.
- ➢ Remove the string and cut the turkey into slices.
- ➢ Place the stuffed turkey slices on serving plates and serve.

Turkey legs with mushrooms and potatoes

PREPARATION TIME: 25 minutes I COOKING TIME: 45 minutes I SERVINGS: 4

- ✓ 2 turkey legs
- ✓ 400 gr of mixed mushrooms
- ✓ 400 gr of potatoes 400
- ✓ 2 cloves of garlic
- ✓ 2 glasses of white wine
- ✓ 1 sprig of thyme
- ✓ 1 sprigs of marjoram

- ✓ Salt and pepper to taste
- ✓ Olive oil to taste

DIRECTIONS

- ➤ Remove the fat and skin from the turkey legs.
- ➤ Wash the turkey legs under running water and then pat them dry with a paper towel.
- ➤ Peel the garlic cloves and spread them over the entire surface of the meat.
- ➤ Peel the potatoes, wash them, and then cut them into wedges.
- ➤ Wash and dry the mushrooms and then cut them into slices.
- ➤ Wash and dry the marjoram and thyme.
- ➤ Brush a baking pan with olive oil and put the turkey legs inside.
- ➤ Add the potatoes, mushrooms, thyme, and marjoram.
- ➤ Season with oil, salt and pepper and sprinkle with white wine.
- ➤ Put the baking pan in the air fryer and cook at 180 ° C for 45 minutes, turning the meat halfway through cooking.
- ➤ After cooking, remove the baking pan from the air fryer.
- ➤ Divide the turkey legs into 4 parts.
- ➤ Add the potatoes and mushrooms and serve.

Turkey meatloaf with orange sauce

PREPARATION TIME: 20 minutes I COOKING TIME: 30 minutes I SERVINGS: 4

- ✓ 500 g of minced turkey breast
- ✓ 30 gr of breadcrumbs
- ✓ 3 sprigs of thyme
- ✓ 2 sprigs of parsley
- ✓ 2 oranges
- ✓ 6 shallots
- ✓ Olive oil to taste
- ✓ Salt and pepper to taste

DIRECTIONS

- ➤ Wash and dry the thyme and parsley, chop them, and put them in a bowl.
- ➤ Add the turkey meat, breadcrumbs, salt, and pepper.
- ➤ Mix until you get a homogeneous mixture.
- ➤ Transfer the dough to a sheet of baking paper, shape it into a meatloaf, wrap it in paper and tie the ends with kitchen twine.
- ➤ Put the meatloaf inside the air fryer and cook at 200 ° C for 30 minutes.
- ➤ Meanwhile, wash and dry the oranges, grate the zest, and put the juice in a bowl.
- ➤ Peel the shallots, cut them into slices and cook them in the pan with boiling olive oil for 5 minutes.
- ➤ Add the juice and zest of the oranges and cook for another 5 minutes.
- ➤ After 5 minutes, season with salt and pepper and turn off.
- ➤ After cooking, remove the meatloaf from the air fryer.
- ➤ Remove the string and parchment paper and cut the meatloaf into slices.
- ➤ Sprinkle with the shallot and orange sauce and serve.

Meat

Beef fillet with basil sauce

PREPARATION TIME: 20 minutes I COOKING TIME: 15 minutes I SERVINGS: 4

- ✓ 800 gr of beef fillet
- ✓ ½ glass of cognac
- ✓ 30 basil leaves
- ✓ 20 g of pine nuts
- ✓ ½ lemon zest
- ✓ 100 ml of cooking cream
- ✓ Olive oil to taste
- ✓ Salt and pepper to taste

DIRECTIONS

- ➢ Remove the excess fat from the fillet and then tie it with kitchen twine.
- ➢ Brush a baking pan with olive oil and put the fillet inside.
- ➢ Season with salt and pepper and then sprinkle with Cognac.
- ➢ Put the baking pan inside the air fryer and cook at 200 ° C for 15 minutes, turning the meat every 5 minutes.
- ➢ Meanwhile, wash the basil leaves and put them in the blender glass.
- ➢ Add the pine nuts, lemon zest, salt, pepper and lemon zest and blend until smooth.
- ➢ Put the mixture with the cream in a saucepan and bring to a boil.
- ➢ Turn off and keep the sauce aside.
- ➢ After cooking, remove the baking pan from the air fryer.
- ➢ Put the beef fillet on a cutting board, remove the string and cut it into slices.
- ➢ Put the fillet on the plates, sprinkle with the basil sauce and serve.

Beef fillet with peppers and Tabasco

PREPARATION TIME: 15 minutes I COOKING TIME: 20 minutes I SERVINGS: 4

- ✓ 800 gr of beef fillet
- ✓ 1 red pepper
- ✓ 1 yellow pepper
- ✓ 1 shallot
- ✓ 1 teaspoon of Tabasco
- ✓ Olive oil to taste
- ✓ Salt and pepper to taste

DIRECTIONS

- ➢ Wash and pat the beef fillet with a paper towel.
- ➢ Massage the meat on both sides with salt and pepper.
- ➢ Wash and chop the shallot.
- ➢ Remove the caps from the peppers and the internal seeds, then cut them into thin strips.
- ➢ Put the meat with the chopped shallot, peppers, and Tabasco in a baking pan suitable for an air fryer.
- ➢ Brush with a little oil and cook for 20 minutes at 200 ° C, turning the beef halfway through cooking.
- ➢ Once cooked, remove the beef fillet from the air fryer and place it on a cutting board.

> cut the beef into slices and then put it on serving plates, surrounded by peppers and shallots.

Breaded lamb chops

PREPARATION TIME: 20 minutes I COOKING TIME: 12 minutes I SERVINGS: 4

- ✓ 16 lamb chops
- ✓ 4 eggs
- ✓ 1 lemon
- ✓ 1 glass of white wine
- ✓ Flour to taste
- ✓ 2 tbsp of chopped thyme
- ✓ Breadcrumbs to taste
- ✓ Salt and pepper to taste
- ✓ Olive oil to taste

DIRECTIONS

> Wash and dry the ribs and remove excess fat.
> Put the cutlets in a bowl and leave them to marinate for 10 minutes with oil, salt, pepper, lemon juice and white wine.
> Break the eggs into a bowl, add salt and pepper and beat them with a fork.
> Put the flour on a plate, add the thyme and mix well.
> Put the breadcrumbs in another bowl.
> Pass the ribs first in the flour, then in the eggs and finally in the breadcrumbs.
> Brush the basket of the air fryer with olive oil and put the ribs inside.
> Sprinkle a little oil and cook at 200 ° C for 12 minutes, turning the meat halfway through cooking.
> Once cooked, take the chops from the air fryer, place them on plates and serve.

Lamb chops with almonds and potatoes

PREPARATION TIME: 20 minutes I COOKING TIME: 25 minutes I SERVINGS: 4

- ✓ 800 gr of lamb chops
- ✓ 400 gr of potatoes
- ✓ 1 clove of garlic
- ✓ 4 tbsp of chopped almonds
- ✓ 1 tbsp of chopped cilantro
- ✓ Salt and pepper to taste
- ✓ Olive oil to taste

DIRECTIONS

> First, proceed with cleaning the lamb chops by rinsing them under running water, then pat them dry with a paper towel.
> Peel, wash and chop the garlic clove.
> Also chop the almonds.
> Marinate your cutlets for 10 minutes with 4 tablespoons of oil, chopped coriander, clove of garlic, pepper, and salt.
> Meanwhile, peel and wash the potatoes, then cut them and cubes.
> Put the lamb chops with the marinade in the air fryer and add the potatoes.
> Season with salt and pepper and close the air fryer.
> Cook them at 180 ° C for 25 minutes.
> Once cooked, take the lamb chops, and place them on serving plates.
> Add the potatoes, sprinkle with almonds, and serve.

Lamb with honey and balsamic vinegar

PREPARATION TIME: 15 minutes I COOKING TIME: 10 minutes I SERVINGS: 4

- ✓ 1 kilo of lamb chops
- ✓ 1 blood orange
- ✓ 2 tbsp of barbecue sauce
- ✓ 2 tbsp of honey
- ✓ 2 tbsp of balsamic vinegar
- ✓ 4 sticks of celery
- ✓ 1 tbsp of chopped parsley
- ✓ Olive oil to taste
- ✓ Salt and pepper to taste

DIRECTIONS

- ➢ First, remove the filaments from the celery, peel it, wash it, and chop it.
- ➢ At the same time, remove all excess fat from the chops and place them in a bowl.
- ➢ Add the celery, salt, pepper, and olive oil.
- ➢ Cover the bowl and marinate for about ten minutes.
- ➢ After 10 minutes, drain the chops and place them in the fryer basket.
- ➢ Cook at 180 ° C for 5 minutes per side.
- ➢ Meanwhile, put the juice of half an orange, the barbecue sauce, honey and balsamic vinegar, a little oil in a bowl and start mixing. Then add the salt, pepper and parsley and mix well.
- ➢ Once cooked, take the chops, and place them on serving plates.
- ➢ Sprinkle with the vinegar and honey sauce and serve.

Lamb with soy

PREPARATION TIME: 20 minutes I COOKING TIME:25 minutes I SERVINGS: 4

- ✓ 600 gr of lamb fillet
- ✓ 2 tomatoes
- ✓ 1 cinnamon stick
- ✓ 1 tbsp of soy sauce
- ✓ 1 onion
- ✓ 375 ml of water
- ✓ Salt and pepper to taste
- ✓ Olive oil to taste

DIRECTION

Remove the excess fat from the lamb fillet and cut into cubes.

- ➢ Put the meat in a bowl and season with oil, soy sauce, salt, and pepper.
- ➢ Mix well and leave to marinate for 15 minutes.
- ➢ Meanwhile, wash the tomatoes and cut them into cubes.
- ➢ Peel the onion and cut it into thin rings.
- ➢ After 15 minutes, brush a baking pan with olive oil and put the onion and tomatoes inside.
- ➢ Season with salt and pepper and then add the lamb, cinnamon, and water.
- ➢ Put the baking pan inside the air fryer and cook at 180 ° C for 20 minutes, stirring the meat every 5 minutes.
- ➢ After cooking, remove the baking pan from the air fryer.
- ➢ Put the lamb, onion, and tomatoes on the plates.
- ➢ Sprinkle with the cooking juices and serve.

Pork chops with honey

PREPARATION TIME: 15 minutes I COOKING TIME: 15 minutes I SERVINGS: 4

- ✓ 4 pork chops of 150 gr each
- ✓ 50 grams of honey
- ✓ 2 tbsp of balsamic vinegar
- ✓ 1 onion
- ✓ 40 gr of butter
- ✓ Salt and pepper to taste
- ✓ Olive oil to taste

DIRECTIONS

- ➢ Peel the onions and then cut them into thin slices.
- ➢ Brush the chops with olive oil, then season with salt and pepper.
- ➢ Put the chops inside the fryer and cook at 200 ° C, 5 minutes per side.
- ➢ Meanwhile, put the butter in the pan and let it melt.
- ➢ Add the onion and cook for 5 minutes.
- ➢ Add the honey, balsamic vinegar, salt, and pepper.
- ➢ Mix well, cook for another 5 minutes, and then turn off.
- ➢ Once cooked, remove the chops from the air fryer.
- ➢ Sprinkle them with the onions and the cooking juices and serve.

Pork loin with potatoes

PREPARATION TIME: 25 minutes I REST TIME: 3 hours I COOKING TIME: 25 minutes I SERVINGS: 4

- ✓ 800 gr of pork loin
- ✓ 400 gr of potatoes
- ✓ 2 onions
- ✓ 1 clove of garlic
- ✓ 2 sprigs of rosemary
- ✓ 4 bay leaves
- ✓ 1 glass of white wine
- ✓ Salt and pepper to taste
- ✓ Olive oil to taste

DIRECTIONS

- ➢ Wash and dry the rosemary and bay leaves and then chop them.
- ➢ Peel and wash the garlic and then chop it.
- ➢ Wash and pat the meat with a paper towel and remove all excess fat.
- ➢ Put the meat in a bowl and add oil, salt, pepper, wine, garlic, bay leaf and chopped rosemary.
- ➢ Cover the bowl with cling film and put the meat to marinate in the fridge for 3 hours.
- ➢ After 3 hours, remove the meat from the fridge and let it rest for a few minutes at room temperature.
- ➢ Meanwhile, peel the potatoes, wash them, and then cut them into wedges.
- ➢ Peel and wash the onions and then cut into slices.
- ➢ Brush the pan with olive oil and put the potatoes and onions inside.
- ➢ Season with oil, salt, and pepper.
- ➢ Put the pork loin on top of the potatoes and put the baking pan inside the air fryer.
- ➢ Cook at 200 ° C for 25 minutes, turning the meat halfway through cooking.
- ➢ After cooking, remove the baking pan from the air fryer and place the pork loin on a cutting board.
- ➢ Cut the meat into slices and place it on serving plates.

➢ Add the potatoes and serve.

Pork loin with walnut sauce

PREPARATION TIME: 20 minutes I COOKING TIME: 30 minutes I SERVINGS: 4

- ✓ 800 gr of pork loin
- ✓ 500 ml of milk
- ✓ 1 glass of white wine
- ✓ 4 tsp of potato starch
- ✓ 2 shallots
- ✓ 2 sprigs of rosemary
- ✓ 100 gr of chopped walnuts
- ✓ Salt and pepper to taste
- ✓ Olive oil to taste

DIRECTIONS

➢ Peel the shallots and then chop them.
➢ Wash and dry the rosemary.
➢ Remove the excess fat from the pork loin and put it in a baking pan brushed with olive oil.
➢ Season with salt and pepper, add the shallots and rosemary and sprinkle with white wine.
➢ Finally, add the milk and put the baking pan inside the air fryer.
➢ Cook at 190 ° C for 20 minutes.
➢ After cooking, remove the baking pan from the air fryer and place the pork loin on a cutting board.
➢ Remove the rosemary and put the cooking juices in a saucepan.
➢ Bring to a boil and then add the potato starch.
➢ Let the sauce thicken, then add the walnuts, mix well, and turn off.

➢ Now cut the pork loin into slices and put them on the plates.
➢ Sprinkle with the walnut sauce and serve.

Roast beef with almond sauce

PREPARATION TIME: 15 minutes I REST TIME: 1 hour I COOKING TIME: 30 minutes I SERVINGS: 4

- ✓ 800 gr of beef for roasts
- ✓ 2 oranges
- ✓ 4 tbsp of ground almonds
- ✓ 3 sprigs of rosemary
- ✓ 10 gr of butter
- ✓ ½ teaspoon of corn flour
- ✓ 1 glass of Cognac
- ✓ Salt and pepper to taste
- ✓ Olive oil to taste

DIRECTIONS

➢ Wash the oranges well.
➢ After washing and drying it, finely grate the peel and then squeeze the juice.
➢ Wash and chop the rosemary sprigs.
➢ Collect the juice and peel of the oranges in a baking dish and add the rosemary, salt, and pepper. Mix the ingredients well.
➢ Clean the meat from any excess fat or waste, then pat it dry with a paper towel.
➢ Now put the meat in the orange and rosemary marinade.
➢ Leave the beef to marinate for an hour, turning it often in the liquid.
➢ After the hour, brush the pan with olive oil and put the roast inside with all the marinade.

- Deglaze with the Cognac and put the baking pan inside the air fryer.
- Cook at 190 ° C for 25 minutes, turning the meat every 10 minutes.
- When cooked, remove the baking pan from the air fryer, put the beef on a cutting board and strain the bottom and then put it in a saucepan.
- Bring to a boil and then add the sifted cornstarch and chopped almonds a spoon.
- Mix well with a fork to avoid the formation of lumps.
- Let the cooking juices thicken, adjusting with salt and pepper if necessary.
- Cut the roast into slices and place it on serving plates.
- Sprinkle with the sauce and serve.

Roast beef with mint and thyme

PREPARATION TIME: 15 minutes I COOKING TIME: 25 minutes I SERVINGS: 4

- ✓ 800 gr of beef rump
- ✓ 10 mint leaves
- ✓ 4 sprigs of thyme
- ✓ 1 shallot
- ✓ 1 glass of white wine
- ✓ 400 ml of beef broth
- ✓ Salt and pepper to taste
- ✓ Olive oil to taste

DIRECTIONS

- First, peel and wash the shallot and cut it into slices.
- Wash both the mint and the thyme.
- Wash and dry the beef and remove excess fat.

- Roll the beef in kitchen twine.
- Brush a baking pan suitable for an air fryer with olive oil and put the beef inside.
- Add the shallot, mint, and thyme.
- Season with oil, salt and pepper and sprinkle with white wine.
- Put the baking pan in the air fryer and cook at 200 ° C for 5 minutes.
- After 5 minutes, turn the veal and add the broth.
- Cook for another 20 minutes.
- Once cooked, remove the beef from the air fryer and let it sit for a couple of minutes.
- Put the beef on a cutting board and remove the kitchen string.
- Cut the roast into slices and place it on serving plates.
- Sprinkle with the cooking juices and serve.

Roast beef with spinach, onions, and pine nuts

PREPARATION TIME: 20 minutes I COOKING TIME: 25 minutes I SERVINGS: 4

- ✓ 700 gr of beef rump
- ✓ 400 gr of spinach
- ✓ 1 onion
- ✓ 4 tbsp of toasted and chopped pine nuts
- ✓ Salt and pepper to taste
- ✓ Olive oil to taste

DIRECTIONS

- Wash and pat the beef with a paper towel and remove excess fat, and season the meat with salt and pepper
- Peel the onion, wash it, and chop it.

- ➤ Wash and dry the spinach and chop too.
- ➤ Put the beef, spinach, and onion in a baking pan suitable for an air fryer.
- ➤ Put the baking powder inside the air fryer and cook at 190 ° C for 25 minutes, turning the meat after 10 minutes.
- ➤ As soon as the beef has finished cooking, take it out of the air fryer.
- ➤ Put the roast on a cutting board and cut it into slices.
- ➤ Put the meat on the plates and add the spinach and onion.
- ➤ Sprinkle the roast with toasted pine nuts and serve.

Roast pork with berries

PREPARATION TIME: 25 minutes I REST TIME: 3 hours I COOKING TIME: 25 minutes I SERVINGS: 4

- ✓ 800 gr of pork loin
- ✓ 1 onion
- ✓ 200 gr of berries
- ✓ 400 ml of vegetable broth
- ✓ 4 sage leaves
- ✓ 1 glass of white wine
- ✓ 4 tablespoons of balsamic vinegar
- ✓ Olive oil to taste
- ✓ Salt and pepper to taste

DIRECTIONS

- ➤ Wash and dry the sage leaves.
- ➤ Wash and dry the pork loin and remove excess fat.
- ➤ Put the pork loin in a bowl.
- ➤ Add oil, salt, pepper, vegetable broth, wine, and sage leaves.
- ➤ Turn the meat a couple of times, then cover the bowl with cling film and put it to marinate in the fridge for 3 hours.

- ➤ After 3 hours, remove the meat from the fridge and put it in a baking pan with all the marinade.
- ➤ Put the baking pan inside the air fryer and cook at 200 ° C for 25 minutes.
- ➤ Meanwhile, peel and wash the onion and then chop it.
- ➤ Wash and dry the berries.
- ➤ Put the berries, onions, and balsamic vinegar in the pan.
- ➤ Put the pan on the stove and cook until the sauce has reduced by half.
- ➤ Once cooked, take an immersion blender and blend until you get a smooth sauce.
- ➤ Once cooked, remove the baking pan from the air fryer and place the meat on a cutting board.
- ➤ Cut the loin and put it on serving plates.
- ➤ Sprinkle with the berry sauce and serve.

Sausage in white wine

PREPARATION TIME: 10 minutes I COOKING TIME: 15 minutes I SERVINGS: 4

- ✓ 600 gr of pork sausage
- ✓ 1 glass of white wine
- ✓ 1 sprig of tarragon
- ✓ 1 sprig of thyme
- ✓ 1 tsp of pink peppercorns

DIRECTIONS

- ➤ Prick the sausage with a fork in several places.
- ➤ Wash and dry the thyme and tarragon and then chop them.
- ➤ Roll the sausage on itself and put it in a baking pan brushed with olive oil.
- ➤ Sprinkle with chopped herbs and pink pepper and place the baking pan inside the air fryer.

- ➤ Cook at 180°C for 5 minutes.
- ➤ After 5 minutes, sprinkle with white wine and continue cooking for another 10 minutes.
- ➤ After cooking, remove the baking pan from the air fryer.
- ➤ Cut the sausage into 4 parts, put it on serving plates and serve.

Sausage with potatoes and peppers

PREPARATION TIME: 20 minutes I COOKING TIME: 20 minutes I SERVINGS: 4

- ✓ 400 gr of sausage
- ✓ 600 gr of potatoes
- ✓ 2 yellow peppers
- ✓ 2 red peppers
- ✓ Salt and pepper to taste
- ✓ Olive oil to taste

DIRECTIONS

- ➤ Peel the potatoes, wash them under running water and then cut them into wedges.
- ➤ Remove the cap from the peppers, the seeds and the white filaments and then cut them into layers.
- ➤ Put the potatoes, peppers, and sausage inside the air fryer.
- ➤ Season with oil, salt and pepper and close the fryer.
- ➤ Cook at 180 ° C for 20 minutes.
- ➤ Once cooked, take the sausage, peppers, and potatoes from the fryer, put them on serving plates and serve.

Spicy Curry Beef Fillet

PREPARATION TIME: 15 minutes I COOKING TIME: 15 minutes I SERVINGS: 4

- ✓ 4 slices of beef fillet of 200 gr each
- ✓ 2 tbsp of curry powder
- ✓ 1 tsp of spicy paprika
- ✓ 20 gr of butter
- ✓ 1 lemon
- ✓ 1 cup of hot vegetable broth
- ✓ 60 ml of cooking cream
- ✓ Salt and pepper to taste
- ✓ Olive oil to taste

DIRECTIONS

- ➤ Remove the excess fat from the beef fillets and tie them with kitchen twine.
- ➤ Brush them with olive oil and season with oil, salt, pepper and spicy paprika.
- ➤ Put the curry in the cup with the hot broth and stir until completely dissolved.
- ➤ Put the meat in a baking pan brushed the meat and sprinkle with the curry broth.
- ➤ Put the baking pan inside the air fryer and cook at 200 ° C for 8 minutes, turning the meat halfway through cooking.
- ➤ After cooking, remove the baking pan from the air fryer.
- ➤ Put the fillets on the plates and remove the string.
- ➤ Put the cooking juices in a saucepan and add the cooking cream and lemon juice.

Fish and seafood

Cod with asparagus

PREPARATION TIME: 25 minutes I COOKING TIME: 15 minutes I SERVINGS: 4

- ✓ 4 cod fillets of 200 gr each
- ✓ 400 gr of asparagus
- ✓ 2 sprigs of parsley
- ✓ 12 basil leaves
- ✓ 3 lemons
- ✓ 200 gr of Greek yogurt
- ✓ Olive oil to taste
- ✓ Salt and pepper to taste

DIRECTIONS

- ➤ Wash and pat the cod fillets with a paper towel and remove skin and bones.
- ➤ Put the filtered lemon juice, salt, pepper and 4 tablespoons of olive oil in a bowl.
- ➤ Stir until you get a homogeneous emulsion.
- ➤ Remove the stalk and the hardest part of the asparagus, then wash and dry them.
- ➤ Put the asparagus in a baking pan and season with salt, pepper, and olive oil.
- ➤ Turn them several times to make them flavour well.
- ➤ Put the cod in the baking pan with the asparagus and season with salt and pepper.
- ➤ Place the pan inside the air fryer and cook at 180°C for 15 minutes, turning the fish halfway through cooking.
- ➤ Meanwhile, wash and dry the parsley and basil and then chop them.
- ➤ Put the yogurt, parsley, basil, oil, salt, and pepper in a bowl and mix well.

- ➤ After cooking, remove the baking from the air fryer.
- ➤ Now put the asparagus on the serving plates.
- ➤ Place the cod fillets on top, sprinkle with the yogurt sauce and serve.

Cod fillet with aubergine and mint

PREPARATION TIME: 20 minutes I COOKING TIME: 20 minutes I SERVINGS: 4

- ✓ 4 cod fillets of 200 gr each
- ✓ 2 aubergines
- ✓ 12 mint leaves
- ✓ Salt and pepper to taste
- ✓ Olive oil to taste

DIRECTIONS

- ➤ Wash and dry the aubergines and cut them into cubes.
- ➤ Put the aubergine cubes in the air fryer.
- ➤ Cook at 180°C for 10 minutes.
- ➤ Once cooked, remove the aubergine cubes from the air fryer and place them on a plate.
- ➤ Wash and dry the cod fillets, removing skin and bones and season them with oil, salt, and pepper.
- ➤ Cook the cod in the deep fryer, cooking at 180 °C for 5 minutes per side.
- ➤ Meanwhile, while the cod is cooking, make the mint sauce.
- ➤ Wash and dry the mint leaves and put them in the blender glass.
- ➤ Add salt, pepper and olive oil and blend until you get a thick and homogeneous sauce.

- ➤ Once cooked, remove the cod from the air fryer and place it on serving plates.
- ➤ Garnish with the aubergine cubes, drizzle with the mint sauce and serve.

Cod with carrots

PREPARATION TIME: 20 minutes I COOKING TIME: 12 minutes I SERVINGS: 4

- ✓ 600 gr of cod fillet
- ✓ 80 gr of breadcrumbs
- ✓ 2 tablespoons of mustard
- ✓ 4 carrots
- ✓ 2 sprigs of parsley
- ✓ 2 cloves of garlic
- ✓ Salt and pepper to taste
- ✓ Olive oil to taste

DIRECTIONS

- ➤ Trim the carrots, peel them, wash them, and then cut them into thin slices.
- ➤ Peel the garlic cloves and then cut them into thin slices.
- ➤ Wash the parsley and then chop it.
- ➤ Put the parsley and garlic in a bowl. Add the breadcrumbs, salt, and pepper, 2 tablespoons of olive oil and mustard, and mix well.
- ➤ Wash the cod fillet, remove the skin and bones, and then cut it into small slices.
- ➤ Brush the cod with a little oil and then pass it into the bowl with the breadcrumbs.
- ➤ Brush a baking pan with oil and put the cod and carrots inside.
- ➤ Season the carrots with oil, salt and pepper and put the baking pan in the fryer.
- ➤ Cook at 180 ° C for 12 minutes, turning the fish halfway through cooking.

- ➤ Once cooked, remove the baking pan from the air fryer, place the cod and carrots on the plates and serve.

Cod with potatoes and olives

PREPARATION TIME: 20 minutes I COOKING TIME: 35 minutes I SERVINGS: 4

- ✓ 600 gr of cod fillet
- ✓ 2 tbsp of pine nuts
- ✓ 4 potatoes
- ✓ 12 black olives
- ✓ 1 glass of white wine
- ✓ 1 clove of garlic
- ✓ 1 tbsp of chopped parsley
- ✓ 1 glass of fish broth
- ✓ Salt and pepper to taste
- ✓ Olive oil to taste

DIRECTIONS

- ➤ Wash and dry the cod fillet, remove the skin and bones, and then cut it into small slices.
- ➤ Peel and wash the potatoes and then cut them into cubes.
- ➤ Put the potatoes in the pan with cold water and salt, bring to a boil and continue cooking for another 15 minutes.
- ➤ After 15 minutes, drain the potatoes and place them in a baking pan, suitable for your air fryer, brushed with olive oil.
- ➤ Peel and chop the garlic clove.
- ➤ Put the cod on top of the potatoes and add the olives as well.
- ➤ Season with oil, salt, and pepper, then sprinkle with the wine, broth, and minced garlic.

- Put the baking pan in the deep fryer and cook at 180°C for 12 minutes, turning the fish halfway through cooking.
- Once cooked, remove the baking pan from the air fryer, and put the cod, potatoes, and olives on the plates.
- Sprinkle with the cooking sauce and chopped parsley and serve.

Fresh tuna salad with mushrooms and fennel

PREPARATION TIME: 20 minutes I COOKING TIME: 8 minutes I SERVNGS: 4

- ✓ 800 gr of tuna fillet
- ✓ 2 oranges
- ✓ 200 gr of Champignon mushrooms
- ✓ 2 fennels
- ✓ Olive oil to taste
- ✓ Salt and pepper to taste

DIRECTIONS

- Wash and pat the tuna fillet with a paper towel.
- Brush the tuna with olive oil and season with salt and pepper.
- Put the tuna fillet inside the air fryer and cook at 180 ° C for 8 minutes.
- Meanwhile, remove the earthy part of the mushrooms, wash them under running water and dry them. Cut them into thin slices and put them in a bowl.
- Remove the beard and the toughest leaves external to the fennel. Wash them, dry them, and then cut them into slices.
- Put the fennel in the bowl with the mushrooms and season with oil, salt, and pepper.

- Once cooked, remove the tuna from the air fryer.
- Put the tuna on a cutting board and cut it into thin slices.
- Put the tuna in the bowl with the mushrooms and fennel.
- Squeeze the oranges and strain the juice into a bowl.
- Add two tablespoons of olive oil, salt and pepper and mix well.
- Sprinkle the salad with the emulsion and serve.

Fried calamari rings with curry breading

PREPARATION TIME: 20 minutes I COOKING TIME: 8 minutes I SERVINGS: 4

- ✓ 4 calamari already cleaned
- ✓ Flour to taste
- ✓ Corn flour to taste
- ✓ 1 tbsp of curry powder
- ✓ Salt and pepper to taste
- ✓ Olive oil to taste

DIRECTIONS

1. Wash and dry the calamari and then cut them into rings.
2. Put the two flours and the curry, salt and pepper on a plate and mix well.
3. Dip the calamari rings in the breadcrumbs and then put them in the fryer basket, brushed with olive oil.
4. Sprinkle a little oil and cook at 200 ° C for 8 minutes, stirring gently halfway through cooking.
5. Once cooked, remove the squid from the fryer, place them on the plates and serve.

Fried coconut prawns with orange sauce

PREPARATION TIME: 20 minutes I COOKING TIME: 4 minutes I SERVINGS: 4

- ✓ 400 gr of prawns
- ✓ 100 gr of rice flour
- ✓ 100 grams of coconut flour
- ✓ 2 eggs
- ✓ 150 gr of orange jam
- ✓ 2 tbsp of mustard
- ✓ Salt and pepper to taste
- ✓ Olive oil to taste

DIRECTIONS

- ➤ Shell the prawns, depriving them of the carapace and the head, but keeping the tail intact.
- ➤ Eliminate the intestinal filament, then wash them and pat them with a paper towel.
- ➤ Break the eggs into a bowl and add salt and pepper. Mix well with a fork.
- ➤ Put the rice and coconut flour on a plate.
- ➤ Pass the prawns first in the eggs and then in the two flours.
- ➤ Brush the basket of the air fryer with olive oil and put the prawns inside.
- ➤ Cook at 180 ° C for 4 minutes, turning the prawns halfway through cooking.
- ➤ Meanwhile, prepare the sauce.
- ➤ Put the orange marmalade, mustard, salt, and pepper in a bowl and mix until you get a homogeneous mixture.
- ➤ When the prawns are ready, remove them from the fryer and place them on the plates.
- ➤ Sprinkle with the orange sauce and serve.

Fried cod

PREPARATION TIME: 15 minutes I COOKING TIME: 10 minutes I SERVINGS: 4

- ✓ 600 gr of cod fillet
- ✓ 200 gr of flour
- ✓ 300 grams of iced sparkling water
- ✓ 1 lemon, sliced
- ✓ Salt and pepper to taste
- ✓ Olive oil to taste

DIRECTIONS

- ➤ Wash and dry the cod and remove all the bones.
- ➤ Cut the cod fillet into smaller pieces.
- ➤ Put the two flours in a bowl and add the sparkling water.
- ➤ Stir until you get a homogeneous and lump-free mixture.
- ➤ Dip the pieces of cod in the batter and coat them well.
- ➤ Remove the excess batter and put the cod in the air fryer.
- ➤ Sprinkle a little oil on the surface and cook at 180 ° C for 10 minutes, turning the fish halfway through cooking.
- ➤ Once cooked, take the cod from the fryer, put it on serving plates, garnish with lemon slices and serve.

King prawns with potatoes

PREPARATION TIME: 20 minutes I REST TIME: 15 minutes I COOKING TIME: 20 minutes I SERVINGS: 4

- ✓ 16 king prawns
- ✓ 4 potatoes
- ✓ 2 tablespoons of balsamic vinegar

- ✓ Olive oil to taste
- ✓ Salt and pepper to taste

DIRECTIONS

- ➢ Peel the potatoes, wash them, and then cut into thin slices.
- ➢ Put the potatoes inside the air fryer.
- ➢ Season with oil, salt, and pepper.
- ➢ Close the air fryer and cook at 180 ° C for 15 minutes.
- ➢ In the meantime, shell the prawns, remove the intestinal filament, wash them, pat them with a paper towel and place them in a bowl.
- ➢ Season with oil, salt and pepper and balsamic vinegar, mix well and let it rest for 15 minutes.
- ➢ After 15 minutes, put the prawns in the air fryer with the potatoes.
- ➢ Cook at 200 ° C for another 5 minutes.
- ➢ Once cooked, take the prawns and potatoes from the air fryer, place them on serving plates and serve.

Octopus salad with cherry tomatoes

PREPARATION TIME: 20 minutes I REST TIME: 30 minutes I COOKING TIME: 40 minutes I SERVINGS: 4

- ✓ 1 kilo of pre-cleaned octopus
- ✓ 100 gr of capers
- ✓ 2 lemons
- ✓ 400 gr of cherry tomatoes
- ✓ 2 sprigs of thyme
- ✓ Salt and pepper to taste
- ✓ Olive oil to taste

DIRECTIONS

- ➢ Squeeze and strain the juice from the lemons into a bowl. Add 4 tablespoons of olive oil, salt and pepper and mix well.
- ➢ Cut the octopus into small pieces and put it in the bowl with the emulsion.
- ➢ Stir to flavour the fish well.
- ➢ Cover the bowl with cling film and leave to marinate for 30 minutes.
- ➢ Wash and dry the thyme.
- ➢ Put the octopus and thyme in the air fryer and cook at 180 ° C for 35 minutes.
- ➢ Once cooked, remove the octopus from the air fryer.
- ➢ Put the octopus in a bowl.
- ➢ Wash and squeeze the capers and put them in the bowl with the octopus.
- ➢ Wash and dry the cherry tomatoes, cut them into 4 parts and put them together with the other ingredients.
- ➢ Season the salad with oil, salt, and pepper, mix everything well, and serve.

Potato crusted sea bream

PREPARATION TIME: 20 minutes I COOKING TIME: 20 minutes I SERVINGS: 4

- ✓ 4 sea bream fillets of 200 gr each
- ✓ 3 medium potatoes
- ✓ Salt and pepper to taste
- ✓ Olive oil to taste

DIRECTIONS

- ➢ Wash the sea bream fillets, pat them with a paper towel and then remove all the bones.
- ➢ Peel the potatoes, wash them several times under running water and then grate them.

- ➢ Put the potatoes in a bowl and season them with oil, salt, and pepper.
- ➢ Brush the sea bream fillets with olive oil, season with salt and pepper and place them in the air fryer.
- ➢ Sprinkle the surface of the sea bream with grated potatoes.
- ➢ Close the air fryer and cook at 180 ° C for 20 minutes.
- ➢ Once cooked, remove the sea bream fillets from the air fryer, place them on serving plates and serve.

Salmon and bacon skewers

PREPARATION TIME: 20 minutes I COOKING TIME: 10 minutes I SERVINGS 4

- ✓ 700 gr of salmon fillet
- ✓ 200 gr of bacon, slices
- ✓ 2 limes
- ✓ Salt and pepper to taste
- ✓ Olive oil to taste

DIRECTIONS

- ➢ Remove the salmon skin and bones and then cut it into cubes.
- ➢ Wash the limes, cut them into rings and then divide the washers into 4 slices.
- ➢ Start putting the skewers together.
- ➢ Put the salmon first, then the lime and finally the bacon.
- ➢ Continue in the same way until the end of the ingredients.
- ➢ Brush the skewers with olive oil and season with salt and pepper.
- ➢ Place the skewers inside the air fryer and cook at 180 ° C for 10, turning the skewers halfway through cooking.

- ➢ Once cooked, remove the skewers from the air fryer, place them on plates and serve.

Salmon au gratin with orange and pistachios

PREPARATION TIME: 20 minutes I COOKING TIME:10 minutes I SERVINGS: 4

- ✓ 4 salmon fillets of 200 gr each
- ✓ 100 gr of breadcrumbs
- ✓ 100 gr of chopped pistachios
- ✓ 2 oranges
- ✓ Salt and pepper to taste
- ✓ Olive oil to taste

DIRECTIONS

- ➢ Wash and dry the salmon fillets and remove the bones.
- ➢ Put the breadcrumbs in a bowl.
- ➢ Wash and dry the oranges, grate the zest, and put them in the bowl with the breadcrumbs.
- ➢ Add the pistachio, salt, pepper, 4 tablespoons of olive oil and mix well.
- ➢ Spread the breading over the salmon and then put it inside the air fryer.
- ➢ Cook at 160 ° C for 5 minutes, then raise the temperature to 180 ° C and continue cooking for another 5 minutes.
- ➢ Once cooked, remove the salmon from the air fryer, place it on plates and serve.

Salmon with basil and aromatic herbs

PREPARATION TIME: 15 minutes I COOKING TIME: 12 minutes I SERVINGS: 4

- ✓ 4 salmon fillets of 200 gr each

- ✓ 1 orange
- ✓ 1 lemon
- ✓ 1 lime
- ✓ 2 sprigs of thyme
- ✓ 2 sprigs of parsley
- ✓ 1 clove of garlic
- ✓ 8 basil leaves
- ✓ 1 glass of white wine
- ✓ Salt and pepper to taste
- ✓ Olive oil to taste

DIRECTIONS

- ➤ Start by washing the orange, lime, and lemon under running water, then remove the peels and strain the juice into a bowl.
- ➤ Wash and dry the thyme, parsley, and basil.
- ➤ Peel and wash the garlic clove, then chop it.
- ➤ Put all the aromatic herbs, orange peel, oil, salt, pepper and garlic in the mixer and chop everything very finely.
- ➤ Wash and dry the salmon and remove all the bones present.
- ➤ brush the salmon with olive oil.
- ➤ Put the salmon fillets inside a baking pan.
- ➤ Season with oil, salt and pepper and then sprinkle it with the citrus juice and white wine.
- ➤ Sprinkle now with the chopped herbs and then put the baking pan inside the air fryer.
- ➤ Cook at 200 ° C for 12 minutes, turning the fish halfway through cooking.
- ➤ After cooking, remove the pan from the air fryer.
- ➤ Put the salmon on serving plates, sprinkle with the cooking juices and serve.

Salmon with lime

PREPARATION TIME: 15 minutes I COOKING TIME: 8 minutes I SERVINGS: 4

- ✓ 4 salmon fillets of 200 gr each
- ✓ 3 limes
- ✓ 4 tbsp of honey
- ✓ Salt and pepper to taste
- ✓ Olive oil to taste

DIRECTIONS

- ➤ Wash and pat the salmon with a paper towel and then remove all the bones.
- ➤ Cut the skin of the fish with a knife and then season with salt and pepper.
- ➤ Put the salmon inside the air fryer from the skin side.
- ➤ Cook at 180 ° C, 4 minutes per side.
- ➤ Meanwhile, put the lime juice, salt, pepper, 4 tablespoons of oil and honey in a bowl.
- ➤ Mix untill you get a homogeneous emulsion.
- ➤ Once cooked, remove the salmon from the air fryer and place it on serving plates.
- ➤ Sprinkle with the lime sauce and serve.

Sea bass with cucumber sauce

PREPARATION TIME: 20 minutes I COOKING TIME: 12 minutes I SERVINGS: 4

- ✓ 4 sea bass fillets of 250 gr each
- ✓ 1 clove of garlic
- ✓ 2 cucumbers
- ✓ 120 ml of orange juice

- ✓ 200 gr of Greek yogurt
- ✓ 1 teaspoon of chopped chives
- ✓ Salt and pepper to taste
- ✓ Olive oil to taste

DIRECTIONS

- ➢ Peel and chop the garlic.
- ➢ Wash and dry the sea bass fillets and remove all the bones present.
- ➢ Season the fillets with oil, salt, and pepper.
- ➢ Brush a baking pan with olive oil.
- ➢ Put the sea bass inside and cover it with the garlic.
- ➢ Place the baking pan inside the air fryer and cook at 200 ° C for 12 minutes.
- ➢ Meanwhile, make the cucumber sauce.
- ➢ Peel the cucumbers, wash them, and cut the pulp into very small pieces.
- ➢ Put the cucumber pulp in the glass of the blender and add the yogurt, oil, salt, and orange juice.
- ➢ Turn on the blender and blend everything, until you get a smooth and homogeneous.
- ➢ Once cooked, remove the sea bass from the air fryer.
- ➢ Put the sea bass on the serving plates.
- ➢ Sprinkle with the cucumber sauce, chopped chives and serve.

Sea bass with lime, orange, and honey

PREPARATION TIME: 25 minutes I COOKING TIME: 12 minutes I SERVINGS: 4

- ✓ 4 sea bass fillets of 250 gr each
- ✓ 4 limes
- ✓ 4 tablespoons of honey
- ✓ 2 oranges
- ✓ Salt and pepper to taste
- ✓ Olive oil to taste

DIRECTIONS

- ➢ Wash and pat the sea bass with a paper towel and remove all the bones.
- ➢ Wash and dry the oranges and limes and cut them into rings.
- ➢ Brush the aluminium foil sheets with olive oil and place the orange and lime slices on top.
- ➢ Put the honey on top of the citrus fruits and finally add the sea bass.
- ➢ Season with oil, salt and pepper and close the packets.
- ➢ Cook at 200 ° C for 12 minutes.
- ➢ After cooking, remove the packets from the air fryer.
- ➢ Let it rest for 5 minutes, then put the packets on the plates.
- ➢ Open them carefully and then serve.

Sea bass with potatoes and mushrooms

PREPARATION TIME: 20 minutes I COOKING TIME: 12 minutes I SERVINGS: 4

- ✓ 4 sea bass fillets of 150 gr each
- ✓ 4 large porcini mushrooms
- ✓ 500 gr of potatoes
- ✓ 1 lime
- ✓ 2 sprigs of rosemary
- ✓ Salt and pepper to taste
- ✓ Olive oil to taste

DIRECTIONS

- ➢ Peel the potatoes, wash them several times under running water and then cut them into slices.
- ➢ Remove the final part of the mushrooms, clean them carefully with a damp cloth and then cut them into pieces.
- ➢ Wash and dry the springs o rosemary.
- ➢ Brush the pan with olive oil and put the potatoes on the bottom.
- ➢ Add the mushrooms and rosemary, season with oil, salt and pepper and put the baking pan in the air fryer.
- ➢ Cook at 180°C for 10 minutes.
- ➢ Meanwhile, wash the sea bass, remove the bones, and place the fillets on a plate.
- ➢ Season them with oil, salt and pepper and the lime juice and leave to flavour for 10 minutes.
- ➢ After 10 minutes, put the sea bass in the baking pan and cook for another 12 minutes.
- ➢ After cooking, remove the baking pan from the air fryer.
- ➢ Put the sea bass, potatoes and mushrooms on the serving plates and serve.

Sea bream with raspberry sauce

PREPARATION TIME: 20 minutes I COOKING TIME: 15 minutes I SERVINGS: 4

- ✓ 4 sea bream fillets of 200 gr each
- ✓ 4 tbsp of balsamic vinegar
- ✓ 100 gr of raspberries
- ✓ Olive oil to taste
- ✓ Salt and pepper to taste

DIRECTIONS

- ➢ Wash and dry the sea bream fillets, then remove all the bones present.
- ➢ Oil the basket of the air fryer and put the fillet inside.
- ➢ Season with oil, salt, and pepper.
- ➢ Cook for 15 minutes at 190 ° C.
- ➢ Meanwhile, wash and dry the raspberries and put them in the glass of the blender together with the vinegar, oil, salt, and pepper.
- ➢ Blend until you get a smooth and homogeneous mixture.
- ➢ After cooking, remove the sea bream fillets from the air fryer.
- ➢ Put the sea bream on the plates, sprinkle with the raspberry sauce and serve.

Prawn meatballs and crab meat

PREPARATION TIME: 20 minutes I COOKING TIME: 12 minutes I SERVINGS: 4

- ✓ 2 boiled potatoes
- ✓ 250 gr of crab meat
- ✓ 250 gr of prawns
- ✓ 2 limes
- ✓ 2 bay leaves
- ✓ 2 sage leaves
- ✓ 4 tbsp of breadcrumbs
- ✓ 1 tbsp of chopped parsley
- ✓ Salt and pepper to taste
- ✓ Olive oil to taste

DIRECTIONS

- ➢ Peel the potatoes, put them in a bowl and mash them with a fork.
- ➢ Chop the crab meat and put it in the bowl with the potatoes.

- Shell the prawns, remove the intestinal filament and then wash them.
- Bring a pot of water, salt, the sliced lime, sage, and bay leaf to a boil and then put the prawns to cook for 4 minutes.
- Once cooked, drain them, pass them under cold water and then chop them.
- Put the prawns in the bowl with the potatoes.
- Add the egg, breadcrumbs, salt, pepper, and parsley and mix well with a fork, until you get a homogeneous mixture.
- Now form several meatballs with the mixture and then place them inside the air fryer.
- Sprinkle with a little oil and cook at 180 ° C for 7 minutes.
- Turn the meatballs, sprinkle a little more oil, and continue cooking for another 5 minutes.
- Once cooked, remove the meatballs from the fryer, put them on plates and serve.

Trout fillet and tomatoes

PREPARATION TIME: 20 minutes I COOKING TIME: 12 minutes I SERVINGS:

- ✓ 4 trout fillets of 200 gr each
- ✓ 1 glass of white wine
- ✓ 4 ripe red tomatoes
- ✓ 2 tsp of dried oregano
- ✓ 2 tbsp of chopped parsley
- ✓ Salt and pepper to taste
- ✓ Olive oil to taste

DIRECTIONS

- Wash and dry the trout fillets, then remove all the bones.
- Wash the tomatoes and then cut them into cubes.

- Brush a baking pan with olive oil and put the trout fillets inside.
- Sprinkle with the tomato, parsley, salt, pepper, and oregano.
- Deglaze with the wine and place the baking pan inside the air fryer.
- Cook at 180° C for 12 minutes.
- After cooking, remove the baking pan from the air fryer.
- Put the trout fillets and tomatoes on the plates.
- Season with the cooking juices and serve.

Trout with almonds

PREPARATION TIME: 25 minutes I COOKING TIME: 12 minutes I SERVINGS: 4

- ✓ 4 salmon trout fillets of 200 gr each
- ✓ 50 gr of toasted almonds
- ✓ 50 gr of butter
- ✓ 2 cloves of garlic
- ✓ 2 tbsp of chopped parsley
- ✓ 1 lemon
- ✓ Salt and pepper to taste
- ✓ Olive oil to taste

DIRECTIONS

- Peel the garlic cloves and then chop them.
- Chop the almonds.
- Wash and pat the trout fillets with a paper towel and remove any bones present.
- Brush the trout fillets with olive oil and season with salt and pepper.
- Put the trout in the air fryer, skin side up and cook for 12 minutes at 180 ° C, turning the fish halfway through cooking.
- Meanwhile, melt the butter and add the lemon juice, garlic, parsley, salt, pepper,

and almonds. Cook for 5 minutes and then turn off.

➢ Once cooked, remove the trout fillets from the fryer and place them on the plates.

➢ Sprinkle with the almond sauce and serve.

➢ Sprinkle some oil on the rolls then place them in the basket of the air fryer.

➢ Cook at 180 ° C for 10 minutes.

➢ Once cooked, remove the rolls from the air fryer, place them on plates and serve.

Tuna and olive rolls

PREPARATION TIME: 20 minutes I COOKING TIME: 15 minutes I SERVINGS: 4

- 400 gr of fresh tuna fillet cut into thin slices
- 40 gr of breadcrumbs
- 4 tbsp of grated Parmesan cheese
- 2 tbsp of chopped parsley
- 12 chopped black olives
- 20 gr of chopped almonds
- Olive oil to taste
- Salt and pepper to taste

DIRECTIONS

➢ Start by preparing the filling. Heat 4 teaspoons of olive oil in the pan.

➢ Add the breadcrumbs and let it cook for 3 minutes, stirring constantly.

➢ Remove the breadcrumbs from the heat and add the Parmesan.

➢ Add the chopped parsley to the breadcrumbs.

➢ Add the olives and the chopped almonds to the breadcrumbs and mix all the ingredients well.

➢ Wash the tuna slices and pat them dry with a paper towel.

➢ Sprinkle each slice of tuna with a little filling and then roll the fish on itself.

➢ Close the rolls with a toothpick.

Vegetarian and vegan

Asparagus with turmeric and ginger

PREPARATION TIME: 20 minutes I COOKING TIME: 20 minutes I SERVINGS: 4

- ✓ 400 gr of asparagus
- ✓ 1 lemon
- ✓ 1 tsp of turmeric powder
- ✓ 1 tsp of ginger powder
- ✓ Salt and pepper to taste
- ✓ Olive oil to taste

DIRECTIONS

- ➤ Wash the asparagus well by removing the hardest part of the stem, about 2 cm, cutting it away.
- ➤ Wash the lemon well, dry it and grate the peel.
- ➤ Take the lemon zest and put it in a bowl.
- ➤ In a saucer put the salt, pepper and turmeric and ginger.
- ➤ Brush the asparagus with olive oil and then pass each asparagus in the spices, to flavour them completely.
- ➤ Put the asparagus to cook directly in the basket of the air fryer at 160 ° C for 20 minutes.
- ➤ After cooking, remove the asparagus from the air fryer.
- ➤ Put the asparagus on serving plates, sprinkle with lemon zest and juice and serve.

Baked sweet potatoes

PREPARATION TIME: 20 minutes I COOKING TIME: 40 minutes I SERVINGS: 4

- ✓ 4 large, sweet potatoes
- ✓ 300 gr of sour cream
- ✓ 2 red tomatoes
- ✓ 2 spring onions
- ✓ 1 bunch of parsley, minced
- ✓ Salt and pepper to taste
- ✓ Olive oil to taste

DIRECTIONS

- ➤ Wash the potatoes under running water and clean the peel by scratching it with a toothbrush, then dry them with a paper towel.
- ➤ Make holes in the edges of the potatoes using the tines of a fork.
- ➤ Brush 4 aluminium sheets with olive oil and put the potatoes inside.
- ➤ Close the packets, place them inside the air fryer and cook at 200 ° C for 40 minutes.
- ➤ Meanwhile, wash the tomatoes and then cut them into cubes.
- ➤ Peel the spring onions, wash them, and then cut them into rings.
- ➤ Once cooked, remove the potatoes from the air fryer.
- ➤ Remove the aluminium foil and place the potatoes on a cutting board.
- ➤ Remove the cap from the potatoes and remove some of the pulp.
- ➤ Put the tomatoes and spring onions inside the potatoes.

- ➢ Season with oil, salt and pepper; spread the parsley and place the potatoes on serving plates.
- ➢ Sprinkle the potatoes with sour cream and serve.

Baskets of potatoes with avocado and cheddar

PREPARATION TIME: 20 minutes I COOKING TIME: 38 minutes I SERVINGS: 4

- ✓ 4 large potatoes
- ✓ 2 tablespoons of chopped walnuts
- ✓ 1 avocado
- ✓ 40 gr of butter
- ✓ 80 grams of grated cheddar
- ✓ Salt and pepper to taste

DIRECTIONS

- ➢ Clean and wash the potatoes in running water, leaving the peel.
- ➢ Arrange them in a pot completely covered with water and salt.
- ➢ Let them cook for about 30 minutes. The potatoes must be quite al dente.
- ➢ Meanwhile, peel the avocado, cut it in half and remove the central stone. Take and wash the avocado pulp and cut it into cubes.
- ➢ When cooked, drain the potatoes, pat them dry with a kitchen towel and then peel them while they are still hot.
- ➢ When they are completely warm, cut the caps of the potatoes lengthwise and set them aside.
- ➢ Scoop the underside of the potato with a spoon to form a cavity large enough to hold an egg.

- ➢ Put 10 grams of butter in each potato boat.
- ➢ Then insert the avocado cubes in the same way and season with a pinch of salt and pepper.
- ➢ Sprinkle each boat with 20 grams of grated cheddar and a little chopped walnut.
- ➢ Cover the baskets with the caps you have set aside.
- ➢ Salt and pepper the caps and brush them with a little melted butter.
- ➢ Place parchment paper of the same size as the basket of the air fryer.
- ➢ Cook at 200 ° C for 8 minutes.
- ➢ If they still don't seem cooked enough, continue cooking for another 2 minutes.
- ➢ Once cooked, remove the potatoes from the air fryer.
- ➢ Put the potatoes on serving plates and serve.

Brussels sprouts with potatoes

PREPARATION TIME: 20 minutes I COOKING TIME: 18 minutes I SERVINGS: 4

- ✓ 600 grams of Brussels sprouts
- ✓ 2 medium potatoes
- ✓ 2 cloves of garlic
- ✓ 1 teaspoon of spicy paprika
- ✓ 2 sprigs of chopped parsley
- ✓ Olive oil to taste
- ✓ Salt and pepper to taste

DIRECTIONS

- ➢ Clean and wash the Brussels sprouts.
- ➢ Peel the potatoes, wash them, and then cut them into cubes.

- Peel the garlic cloves and then chop them.
- Brush a baking pan with olive oil and put the potatoes and Brussels sprouts inside.
- season with oil, salt and pepper and sprinkle with garlic and parsley.
- Put the baking pan inside the air fryer and cook at 200 ° C for 18 minutes.
- After cooking, remove the baking pan from the air fryer.
- Put the Brussels sprouts and potatoes on serving plates and serve.

Carrots with cherry tomatoes and red onion

PREPARATION TIME: 20 minutes I COOKING TIME: 15 minutes I SERVINGS: 4

- ✓ 2 carrots
- ✓ 8 cherry tomatoes
- ✓ 1 red onion
- ✓ Flour to taste
- ✓ 4 mint leaves
- ✓ Olive oil to taste
- ✓ Salt and pepper to taste

DIRECTIONS

- Wash the cherry tomatoes and slice them.
- Peel and wash the carrots and cut them into slices horizontally.
- Wash and slice the red onion.
- Put the vegetables in a bowl and add the flour.
- Mix the vegetables well to distribute the flour evenly.

- Place the carrots with cherry tomatoes and onions in a baking pan suitable for the air fryer.
- Season with oil, salt and pepper and add the mint.
- Put the baking pan in the air fryer and cook at 190 ° C for 15 minutes.
- After cooking, remove the baking pan from the air fryer.
- Put the carrots, cherry tomatoes and onion on the serving plates and serve.

Cheddar croquettes

PREPARATION TIME: 15 minutes I COOKING TIME: 6 minutes I SERVINGS: 4

- ✓ 300 grams of cheddar
- ✓ 50 grams of flour
- ✓ 90 gr of breadcrumbs
- ✓ 2 eggs
- ✓ 2 tbsp milk
- ✓ Salt and pepper to taste
- ✓ Olive oil to taste

DIRECTIONS

- Cut the cheese into rather large pieces, put them in a bowl, sprinkle them with the milk and mix to flavour all the pieces well.
- Put the flour in one dish and the breadcrumbs in another.
- Put the eggs in a bowl, add salt and pepper and beat them in a fork.
- Pass the cheese first in the flour, then in the eggs and finally in the breadcrumbs.
- Brush the basket of the air fryer with olive oil and put the cheese inside.
- Sprinkle a little oil on the surface and cook at 200 ° C for 3 minutes per side.
- Once cooked, remove the cheese from the air fryer, place it on plates and serve.

Cheese onion rings

PREPARATION TIME: 20 minutes I COOKING TIME: 10 minutes I SERVINGS: 4

- ✓ 3 large onions
- ✓ 150 grams of cheddar
- ✓ 130 grams of flour
- ✓ 200 ml of cold sparkling water
- ✓ Breadcrumbs to taste
- ✓ Salt and pepper to taste
- ✓ Olive oil to taste

DIRECTIONS

- ➢ Peel the onions and then cut them into large rings, being careful not to break them.
- ➢ Cut the cheddar into strips.
- ➢ Couple the rings by joining one larger and the other slightly smaller.
- ➢ Pass a strip of cheese through the space between the two rings.
- ➢ Put the flour in a bowl and add the sparkling water.
- ➢ Add salt and pepper and mix until you get a smooth and lump-free mixture.
- ➢ Put the breadcrumbs on a plate.
- ➢ Dip the onion rings first in the batter and then in the breadcrumbs.
- ➢ Brush the basket of the air fryer with olive oil and put the onion rings inside.
- ➢ Sprinkle a little oil and cook at 200 ° C for 10 minutes.
- ➢ Once cooked, take the onion rings from the fryer, place them on plates and serve.

Courgettes and feta croquettes

PREPARATION TIME: 20 minutes I COOKING TIME: 10 minutes I SERVINGS: 4

- ✓ 350 grams of courgettes
- ✓ 120 gr of feta cheese
- ✓ 1 egg
- ✓ 60 grams of flour
- ✓ 1 shallot
- ✓ Dill to taste
- ✓ 80 grams of Greek yogurt
- ✓ Salt and pepper to taste
- ✓ Olive oil to taste

DIRECTIONS

- ➢ Wash the courgettes and grate them in a bowl.
- ➢ Add the egg, salt and pepper and mix well.
- ➢ Crumble the feta and add it to the mixture.
- ➢ Peel and chop the shallot and put it in the bowl with the mixture.
- ➢ Also add the dill and flour and mix well until you get a homogeneous mixture.
- ➢ Put the bowl in the fridge and let it rest for 30 minutes.
- ➢ After 30 minutes, take the mixture out of the fridge and form flattened meatballs.
- ➢ Brush the basket of the air fryer with olive oil and place the croquettes inside.
- ➢ Sprinkle a little oil on the surface and cook at 200 ° C, 5 minutes per side.
- ➢ After cooking, take the croquettes from the air fryer, place them on plates and serve.

Courgettes with maple syrup and ginger

PREPARATION TIME: 15 minutes I COOKING TIME: 15 minutes I SERVINGS: 4

- ✓ 2 large courgettes
- ✓ 2 tbsp of maple syrup
- ✓ 1 tsp of ginger powder
- ✓ Salt and pepper to taste
- ✓ Olive oil to taste

DIRECTIONS

- ➢ Trim the courgettes and then wash them.
- ➢ Then cut them into sticks of almost equal size.
- ➢ Sprinkle the courgette sticks with a few drops of oil and then put them in the air fryer.
- ➢ Cook at 180°C for 15 minutes, turning the courgettes halfway through cooking.
- ➢ Put the maple syrup, ginger, 2 tablespoons of olive oil, salt and pepper in a bowl and mix well.
- ➢ Once cooked, take the courgettes out of the air fryer, and place them on serving plates.
- ➢ Sprinkle the courgettes with the maple syrup and ginger sauce and serve.

Fennel au gratin with shallots and cheddar

PREPARATION TIME: 20 minutes I COOKING TIME: 23 minutes I SERVINGS: 4

- ✓ 2 shallots
- ✓ 4 fennels
- ✓ 200 ml of béchamel
- ✓ 40 grams of grated cheddar
- ✓ 30 gr of butter
- ✓ Salt and pepper to taste

DIRECTIONS

- ➢ Remove the green sprigs and the fennel beard, wash, and dry them.
- ➢ Bring a pot of salted water to a boil. When it comes to a boil, add the fennel, and cook for 15 minutes.
- ➢ Meanwhile, switch to the shallots. Peel and wash them in running water, then slice them.
   Drain the fennels, let them cool and then cut them into wedges.
- ➢ Now put the fennel and shallots in a baking pan suitable for the air fryer.
- ➢ Oil the pan, make a layer of fennel and shallots and put a little béchamel on top.
- ➢ Make a second layer and cover with the béchamel.
- ➢ Then sprinkle the surface of the béchamel with the cheddar and the butter cut into chunks.
- ➢ Put the basket in the fryer set at 200 ° C and for 8 minutes.
- ➢ Always check the cooking and if you are not satisfied you can let it cook for another couple of minutes.
- ➢ After cooking, remove the baking pan from the air fryer.
- ➢ Put the fennel au gratin on serving plates and serve.

Fried potato chips

PREPARATION TIME: 30 minutes I COOKING TIME: 10 minutes I SERVINGS: 4

- ✓ 600 gr of potatoes
- ✓ Salt and pepper to taste
- ✓ Olive oil to taste

DIRECTIONS

➢ Peel the potatoes and wash them carefully under running water.
➢ Cut the potatoes into very thin slices, about 1 mm thick.
➢ Gradually dip the slices in a bowl full of cold water so that they lose some of the starch.
➢ Drain them from the water and pat them gently with a paper towel.
➢ Brush the basket of the air fryer and put the potatoes inside.
➢ Season them with oil, salt and pepper and close the basket.
➢ Cook at 200 ° C for 10 minutes, turning the potatoes gently halfway through cooking.
➢ Once cooked, take the fries out of the air fryer, place them on plates and serve.

Fried potatoes with cheddar and bacon

PREPARATION TIME: 20 minutes I COOKING TIME: 30 minutes I SERVINGS: 4

✓ 600 gr of potatoes
✓ 150 gr of cheddar
✓ 100 gr of sliced bacon
✓ Salt and pepper to taste
✓ Olive oil to taste

DIRECTIONS

➢ Peel the potatoes and wash them under running water.
➢ Cut the potatoes to form many small sticks.
➢ Brush the basket of the air fryer with olive oil and place the potatoes.

➢ Season them with oil, salt and pepper and cook at 200 ° C for 20 minutes, shaking the basket every 5 minutes and sprinkling more oil if necessary.
➢ Meanwhile, grate the cheddar and place it in a bowl.
➢ When the fries are cooked, remove them from the fryer and set aside momentarily.
➢ Put the pan with the cheddar in the deep fryer and cook at 200 ° C for 5 minutes.
➢ Remove the cheddar and add the bacon.
➢ Cook, always at 200 ° C, two minutes per side.
➢ Remove the bacon from the fryer, place it on a cutting board and cut it into small pieces.
➢ Place the fries on the plates, sprinkle with the bacon and melted cheddar and serve.

Herb fried potatoes

PREPARATION TIME: 20 minutes I COOKING TIME: 20 minutes I SERVINGS: 4

✓ 1 kilo of potatoes
✓ 2 sprigs of rosemary
✓ 8 sage leaves
✓ 2 sprigs of thyme
✓ 1 tbsp of chopped chives
✓ Salt and pepper to taste
✓ Olive oil to taste

DIRECTIONS

➢ Peel the potatoes, wash them, and then cut them into sticks.
➢ Dip the sticks in a bowl of cold water to remove excess starch.
➢ Drain them and then dry them with a kitchen towel.

- Wash and dry sage, rosemary and thyme and then chop them.
- Brush the basket of the air fryer with olive oil and put the potatoes inside.
- Season with oil, salt, pepper and aromatic herbs and mix well.
- Cook at 200 ° C for 2 minutes, stirring the potatoes every 5 minutes.
- Once cooked, take the chips from the air fryer, place them on plates and serve.

Japanese fried tofu

PREPARATION TIME: 15 minutes I COOKING TIME: 15 minutes I SERVINGS: 4

- ✓ 400 gr of tofu
- ✓ 7 tbsp of corn starch
- ✓ 4 tbsp of olive oil
- ✓ 20 gr of fresh ginger
- ✓ 2 minced garlic cloves
- ✓ 3 tbsp of soy sauce
- ✓ 2 tbsp of apple cider vinegar
- ✓ 1 tbsp of brown sugar
- ✓ 120 ml of water
- ✓ 2 shallots
- ✓ 4 tbsp of sesame seeds

DIRECTIONS

- Drain the tofu, pat it dry with a paper towel and then cut it into cubes.
- Put 6 tablespoons of cornstarch on a plate and then flour the tofu cubes.
- Pour 3 tablespoons of olive oil into a baking pan and put the tofu cubes inside.
- Put the baking pan in the air fryer and cook at 180 ° C for 6 minutes, turning the tofu halfway through cooking.
- Meanwhile, prepare the sauce.

- Peel the shallots, wash them, and then chop them.
- Heat 1 tablespoon of olive oil in the pan and then add the garlic and shallots.
- Sauté for a couple of minutes and then add the soy sauce, apple cider vinegar, ginger, brown sugar, and mix.
- Put the remaining corn starch in a glass of water, let it melt and then pour it into the pan.
- Stir constantly to avoid lumps and let the sauce thicken completely.
- After cooking, remove the tofu from the air fryer.
- Put the tofu on the serving plates, sprinkle with the sauce and sesame seeds and serve.

Orange beans with mustard sauce

PREPARATION TIME: 20 minutes I COOKING TIME: 18 minutes I SERVINGS: 4

- ✓ 600 gr of green beans
- ✓ 1 orange
- ✓ 1 tsp of spicy paprika
- ✓ 1 tsp of onion powder
- ✓ Salt and black pepper to taste
- ✓ Olive oil to taste
- ✓ For the mustard sauce:
- ✓ 2 tbsp of mustard
- ✓ ½ tsp of mustard seeds
- ✓ 1 tsp of lemon juice
- ✓ Salt and pepper to taste

DIRECTIONS

- Trim the green beans and then wash them under running water.

- Wash the orange well, dry it and grate the zest.
- Take the orange zest and put it in a bowl.
- In a saucer put together the salt, pepper, onion powder and paprika.
- Pass the green beans in the spices, to flavour them completely.
- Put the green beans inside the air fryer and cook at 180 ° C for 18 minutes, turning them from time to time and sprinkling a little olive oil.
- Meanwhile, prepare the mustard sauce, mixing all the ingredients well in a bowl, until you get a homogeneous mixture.
- Once cooked, take the green beans from the air fryer, and place them on serving plates.
- Sprinkle the green beans with the mustard sauce and serve.

Potatoes stuffed with onions

PREPARATION TIME: 20 minutes I COOKING TIME: 20 minutes I SERVINGS: 4

- ✓ 4 boiled potatoes
- ✓ 4 red onions
- ✓ 1 tbsp of chopped chives
- ✓ Salt and pepper to taste
- ✓ Olive oil to taste

DIRECTIONS

- Put the potatoes on a cutting board and slice them on the surface without going too far with the blade.
- Make cuts about 3 mm apart and finish one centimetre from the base of the potato.

- Peel the onions and then cut them into thin slices. Then divide the washers in two.
- Insert the onion half-moons into the potato cuts, to obtain alternating slices of potatoes and onions.
- Push each onion slice down so that it adheres well to the potato and is not pushed out during cooking.
- Put the potatoes inside the air fryer and season with oil, salt, and pepper.
- Sprinkle with chives and cook at 200 ° C for 20 minutes.
- Once cooked, take the potatoes and onions from the air fryer, place them on serving plates and serve.

Potatoes with beer

PREPARATION TIME: 20 minutes I COOKING TIME: 20 minutes I SERVINGS: 4

- ✓ 800 gr of potatoes
- ✓ 150 ml of lager beer
- ✓ 2 sprigs of rosemary
- ✓ 5 sage leaves
- ✓ 1 clove of minced garlic
- ✓ Salt and pepper to taste
- ✓ Olive oil to taste

DIRECTIONS

- Peel the potatoes, wash them, and then cut them into cubes.
- Wash and dry the rosemary.
- Brush a baking pan with olive oil and put the potatoes and rosemary inside.
- Season the potatoes with oil, salt and pepper and then sprinkle them with garlic and beer.
- Put the baking pan inside the air fryer and cook at 180°C for 20 minutes,

turning the potatoes halfway through cooking.
- ➢ After cooking, remove the baking pan from the air fryer.
- ➢ Put the potatoes sprinkled with the cooking juices on the plates and serve.

Sweet and sour tofu

PREPARATION TIME: 20 minutes I COOKING TIME: 15 minutes I SERVINGS: 4

- ✓ 100 gr of yellow peppers
- ✓ 2 red onions
- ✓ 300 grams of tofu
- ✓ 200 ml of sweet and sour sauce
- ✓ 2 tbsp of soy sauce
- ✓ 200 ml of chicken broth
- ✓ 1 tbsp of brown sugar
- ✓ 1 tsp of potato starch
- ✓ Olive oil to taste
- ✓ Salt and pepper to taste

DIRECTIONS

- ➢ Dab the tofu with a paper towel, place it on a cutting board and cut it into cubes of about 1.5 cm per side.
- ➢ Remove the cap from the peppers and remove the white filaments and the seeds from the peppers.
- ➢ Wash the peppers and then cut them into slices.
- ➢ Peel the onions and then cut them into slices.
- ➢ Put the onions, peppers, and tofu inside the air fryer.
- ➢ Season with oil, salt and pepper and cook at 190 ° C for 10 minutes.
- ➢ Meanwhile, prepare the sauce.
- ➢ Melt the potato starch in half a glass of water.

- ➢ Put the chicken broth, soy sauce, sugar, sweet and sour sauce, and potato starch in a saucepan.
- ➢ Cook until the sauce has completely thickened.
- ➢ After cooking, remove the tofu from the air fryer.
- ➢ Put the tofu and vegetables on serving plates.
- ➢ Sprinkle with the sweet and sour sauce and serve.

Tempeh with hot peppers

PREPARATION TIME: 15 minutes I COOKING TIME: 15 minutes I SERVINGS: 4

- ✓ 500 gr of tempeh
- ✓ 2 cloves of garlic
- ✓ 1 red pepper
- ✓ 1 chopped red pepper
- ✓ 1 sprig of chopped parsley
- ✓ Salt and pepper to taste
- ✓ Olive oil to taste

DIRECTIONS

- ➢ Remove the pepper cap, remove the seeds, and white filaments. Wash the pepper and then cut it into cubes.
- ➢ Peel the garlic cloves and then chop them.
- ➢ Cut the tempeh into cubes.
- ➢ Brush the pan with olive oil and put the tempeh and pepper inside.
- ➢ Season with oil, salt and pepper and then sprinkle with garlic and chopped chilli.
- ➢ Put the baking pan in the air fryer and cook at 180° C for 15 minutes.
- ➢ After cooking, remove the baking pan from the air fryer.

- ➤ Put the tempeh and the pepper on the serving plates and serve.

Tofu and mushroom with curry

PREPARATION TIME: 15 minutes I COOKING TIME: 10 minutes I SERVINGS: 4

- ✓ 200 gr of tofu
- ✓ 200 gr of champignon mushrooms
- ✓ 1 tbsp of chopped parsley
- ✓ 250 ml of vegetable broth
- ✓ 1 clove of garlic
- ✓ 2 tsp of curry powder
- ✓ Olive oil to taste
- ✓ Salt and pepper to taste

DIRECTIONS

- ➤ Peel and wash the garlic, then chop it.
- ➤ Remove the earthy part of the mushrooms, wash them, dry them, and cut them into slices.
- ➤ Rinse and pat the tofu with a paper towel and then cut it into cubes.
- ➤ Brush a baking pan with olive oil and put the mushrooms inside.
- ➤ Add the tofu, chopped parsley, curry, olive oil, salt and pepper and mix well.
- ➤ Pour in a little broth and put the baking pan in the air fryer.
- ➤ Cook at 190 ° C for 10 minutes.
- ➤ After cooking, remove the baking pan from the air fryer.
- ➤ Put the tofu and mushrooms on serving plates, sprinkle with the cooking juices and serve.

Tofu with sesame

PREPARATION TIME: 15 minutes I REST TIME: 30 minutes I COOKING TIME: 15 minutes I SERVINGS: 4

- ✓ 500 gr of natural tofu
- ✓ 2 tbsp of sesame seeds
- ✓ 2 tablespoons of mustard
- ✓ 50 ml of seed oil
- ✓ 50 ml of soy sauce
- ✓ 1 tsp of grated fresh ginger
- ✓ 1 lemon

DIRECTIONS

- ➤ Dab the tofu with a paper towel and cut it into sticks.
- ➤ Put the mustard, seed oil, soy sauce, ginger, and filtered lemon juice in a bowl.
- ➤ Mix well and then put the tofu inside.
- ➤ Turn the tofu a couple of times, then put the bowl in the fridge and marinate for 30 minutes.
- ➤ After 30 minutes, take the tofu from the fridge and put the sesame seeds on a plate.
- ➤ Pass the tofu over the sesame seeds and then put it inside the air fryer.
- ➤ Cook at 180 ° C for 15 minutes, turning the tofu sticks every 5 minutes.
- ➤ Once cooked, remove the tofu sticks from the air fryer, place them on serving plates and serve.

Rice and pasta

Baked rice with tomato and mozzarella

PREPARATION TIME: 20 minutes I COOKING TIME: 28 minutes I SERVINGS: 4

- ✓ 240 gr of rice
- ✓ 500 gr of already cooked tomato sauce
- ✓ 150 gr of mozzarella
- ✓ 50 gr of grated Parmesan cheese
- ✓ 30 gr of butter
- ✓ Salt and pepper to taste
- ✓ Olive oil to taste

DIRECTIONS

- ➢ Cook the rice in boiling salted water for 10 minutes, drain and pass it under cold water.
- ➢ Put the rice in a bowl, season it with a little oil and mix.
- ➢ Add the tomato sauce, a pinch of pepper and mix again.
- ➢ Cut the mozzarella into cubes and put it in the bowl with the rice.
- ➢ Add the Parmesan, mix well and then pour the rice into a baking pan brushed with olive oil.
- ➢ Sprinkle the surface of the rice with the butter cut into chunks and place the baking pan inside the air fryer.
- ➢ Cook at 200 ° C for 18 minutes.
- ➢ After cooking, remove the baking pan from the air fryer.
- ➢ Divide the rice into serving plates and serve.

Lasagna with bacon and mushrooms

PREPARATION TIME: 25 minutes I COOKING TIME: 20 minutes I SERVINGS: 4

- ✓ 160 gr of lasagna
- ✓ 1 litre of béchamel
- ✓ 200 gr of sliced bacon
- ✓ 280 gr of cheddar
- ✓ 1 clove of garlic
- ✓ 1 sprig of chopped parsley
- ✓ 500 gr of champignon mushrooms
- ✓ 30 gr of grated Parmesan cheese
- ✓ Olive oil to taste
- ✓ Salt and pepper to taste

DIRECTIONS

- ➢ Remove the earthy part of the mushrooms, then wash and dry them and cut them into thin slices.
- ➢ Peel the garlic and then chop it.
- ➢ Put the mushrooms in a bowl and add the garlic, salt, pepper, olive oil and chopped parsley and mix well.
- ➢ Take a baking pan and brush it with olive oil.
- ➢ Put a little béchamel on the bottom and then put a layer of lasagna on top.
- ➢ Then add the bacon, mushrooms, and diced cheddar.
- ➢ Put another layer of lasagna on top and put the béchamel on top.
- ➢ Proceed as with the previous layer and do the same until the end of the ingredients.

- ➢ Finished with a layer of lasagna, cover with the béchamel and then sprinkle with grated Parmesan.
- ➢ Cook at 180 ° C for 20 minutes.
- ➢ After cooking, remove the baking pan from the air fryer.
- ➢ Divide the lasagna into 4 parts, place them on plates and serve.

Lasagna with potatoes and truffles

PREPARATION TIME: 25 minutes I COOKING TIME: 35 minutes I SERVINGS: 4

- ✓ 250 gr of lasagna
- ✓ 400 gr of boiled potatoes
- ✓ 30 gr of black truffle
- ✓ 300 gr of fresh cheese
- ✓ 250 ml of milk
- ✓ 40 gr of grated Parmesan cheese
- ✓ 20 gr of butter
- ✓ Salt and pepper to taste

DIRECTIONS

- ➢ Peel the potatoes and cut them into thin slices.
- ➢ Peel and wash the truffle and then put it in the glass of the blender.
- ➢ Add the milk, fresh cheese, salt and pepper and blend until smooth and homogeneous.
- ➢ Brush a baking pan with olive oil.
- ➢ Put a layer of lasagna on the bottom, then the truffle cream and finally the potatoes.
- ➢ Continue in the same way until the end of the ingredients and finish with a layer of lasagna and the truffle cream.

- ➢ Sprinkle with Parmesan and put the baking pan inside the air fryer.
- ➢ Cook at 180°C for 35 minutes.
- ➢ After cooking, remove the baking pan from the air fryer.
- ➢ Divide the lasagna into 4 portions, place them on plates and serve.

Lasagna with prawns and courgettes

PREPARATION TIME: 25 minutes I COOKING TIME: 30 minutes I SERVINGS: 4

- ✓ 280 gr of lasagna
- ✓ 2 courgettes
- ✓ 400 gr of prawns
- ✓ 800 ml of béchamel
- ✓ 1 tbsp of chopped thyme
- ✓ 3 tbsp of grated Parmesan cheese
- ✓ Salt and pepper to taste
- ✓ Olive oil to taste

DIRECTIONS

- ➢ Peel the courgettes, wash them, and then cut them into cubes.
- ➢ Shell the prawns, remove the intestinal filament and then wash and pat them with a paper towel.
- ➢ Put the courgettes and prawns in a bowl and season with oil, salt, pepper, and thyme and mix well.
- ➢ Brush a baking pan with olive oil.
- ➢ Put a layer of béchamel on the bottom of the baking pan
- ➢ Put a layer of lasagna on top, then put another layer of béchamel on top.
- ➢ Then put the courgettes and prawns.
- ➢ Proceed in the same way until the end of the ingredients.

- Finish with a layer of lasagna and finally put the béchamel on top.
- Sprinkle with Parmesan cheese and put the baking powder inside the air fryer.
- Cook at 180 ° C for 30 minutes.
- After cooking, remove the baking pan from the air fryer.
- Cut the lasagna into 4 portions, put them on serving plates and serve.

Lasagna with tomatoes and mozzarella

PREPARATION TIME: 25 minutes I COOKING TIME: 20 minutes I SERVINGS: 4

- ✓ 400 gr of lasagna
- ✓ 5 ripe red tomatoes
- ✓ 250 g of mozzarella
- ✓ 2 tbsp of grated Parmesan cheese
- ✓ 4 basil leaves
- ✓ Olive oil to taste
- ✓ Salt and pepper to taste

DIRECTIONS

- Wash the tomatoes, cut them into slices and put them in a bowl.
- Season them with oil, salt and pepper and the basil leaves and leave to marinate for 10 minutes.
- Brush a baking pan with olive oil and put a layer of lasagna on the bottom.
- Put the tomato on top and then the mozzarella.
- Proceed in the same way until the end of the ingredients.
- The last layer must be made up of lasagna.

- Sprinkle the surface of the lasagna with Parmesan and sprinkle with a little olive oil.
- Put the baking pan inside the air fryer and cook at 180 ° C for 20 minutes.
- After cooking, remove the baking pan from the air fryer.
- Divide the lasagna into 4 portions, put them on serving plates and serve.

Pumpkin and sausage lasagna

PREPARATION TIME: 25 minutes I COOKING TIME: 55 minutes I SERVINGS: 4

- ✓ 400 gr of lasagna
- ✓ 400 gr of pumpkin pulp
- ✓ 4 sausages
- ✓ ½ glass of white wine
- ✓ Butter to taste
- ✓ 200 gr of grated Parmesan cheese
- ✓ 800 ml of béchamel
- ✓ Olive oil to taste
- ✓ Salt and pepper to taste

DIRECTIONS

- Wash the pumpkin pulp and then cut it into cubes.
- Remove the skin from the sausage, shell it and put it in a non-stick pan.
- Deglaze with the white wine and cook for 15 minutes.
- Put the pumpkin pulp in the air fryer and season with oil, salt, and pepper.
- Cook at 200 ° C for 20 minutes.
- Once the pumpkin is cooked, remove it from the air fryer, place it in a bowl and mash it with a fork.
- Add the sausage and mix well.

- ➢ Take a baking pan and brush it with olive oil.
- ➢ Put a layer of béchamel on the bottom and then put a layer of lasagna on top.
- ➢ Put the pumpkin and the sausage on top of the lasagna, put a layer of lasagna and then the béchamel on top.
- ➢ Continue in the same way until the end of the ingredients.
- ➢ The last layer must end with the lasagna and béchamel.
- ➢ Cover the entire surface with Parmesan cheese and place the baking pan inside the air fryer.
- ➢ Cook at 180°C for 35 minutes.
- ➢ After cooking, remove the baking pan from the air fryer.
- ➢ Divide the lasagna into 4 portions, put them on serving plates and serve.

Rice Pilaf

PREPARATION TIME: 15 minutes I COOKING TIME: 30 minutes I SERVINGS: 4

- ✓ 340 gr of cooked long grain rice
- ✓ ½ onion
- ✓ 2 tbsp of butter 2
- ✓ 1 tbsp of saffron
- ✓ 500 ml of hot meat broth
- ✓ Salt and pepper to taste
- ✓ Olive oil to taste

DIRECTIONS

- ➢ Peel the onion and then chop it.
- ➢ Put the broth in a bowl and add the saffron.
- ➢ Stir until completely dissolved.
- ➢ Now add the rice, season with salt and pepper, and mix well.

- ➢ Brush a baking pan with olive oil and put the rice inside.
- ➢ Sprinkle the surface of the rice with the butter cut into chunks.
- ➢ Put the baking pan inside the air fryer and cook at 200 ° C for 30 minutes.
- ➢ After cooking, remove the baking pan from the air fryer.
- ➢ Divide the rice into serving plates and serve.

Rice timbale with courgettes

PREPARATION TIME: 25 minutes I COOKING TIME: 30 minutes I SERVINGS: 4

- ✓ 400 gr of rice
- ✓ 1 tbsp of saffron
- ✓ 4 courgettes
- ✓ 1 shallot
- ✓ 2 eggs
- ✓ 30 gr of butter
- ✓ 90 gr of grated Parmesan cheese
- ✓ 200 gr of mozzarella
- ✓ Breadcrumbs to taste
- ✓ Salt and pepper to taste
- ✓ Olive oil to taste

DIRECTIONS

- ➢ Bring plenty of salted water to a boil in a saucepan, add the saffron, let it melt and then pour in the rice. Cook for 15 minutes.
- ➢ Peel the shallot and then cut it into thin slices.
- ➢ Peel the courgettes, wash them, and then cut them into rounds.
- ➢ Put the zucchini and shallot in the air fryer.

- Season with oil, salt and pepper and cook for 10 minutes at 180 ° C.
- When the courgettes are cooked, remove them from the air fryer and place them on a plate.
- Once the rice is cooked, drain it, and put it in a bowl.
- Add the Parmesan, butter, and eggs and mix everything well with a wooden spoon.
- Take a baking pan and brush it with olive oil.
- Put a layer of rice on the bottom and then put the sliced mozzarella on top.
- Then put the courgettes on top and finally another layer of mozzarella.
- Cover with the rest of the rice and sprinkle the surface with breadcrumbs.
- Put the baking pan inside the air fryer and cook at 200 ° C for 15 minutes.
- After cooking, remove the baking pan from the air fryer.
- Divide the timbale into 4 parts, put it on serving plates and serve.

Tagliatelle flan with bacon and cheese

PREPARATION TIME: 25 minutes I COOKING TIME: 35 minutes I SERVINGS: 4

- ✓ 240 gr of tagliatelle
- ✓ 80 gr of smoked bacon
- ✓ 80 gr of grated Gruyere cheese
- ✓ 100 gr of cheddar
- ✓ 2 litres of milk
- ✓ 4 eggs
- ✓ ½ teaspoon of paprika
- ✓ Butter to taste
- ✓ Salt and pepper to taste

DIRECTIONS

- Put the milk in a saucepan and add salt and pepper.
- Bring to a boil and then put the tagliatelle to cook for 8 minutes.
- Drain the tagliatelle and put them in a bowl.
- In another bowl, put the milk you used to cook the tagliatelle, gruyere, diced cheddar, paprika and eggs and mix well.
- Pour the mixture over the tagliatelle, add the diced bacon, and mix everything well.
- Brush a baking pan with olive oil and pour the tagliatelle inside.
- Sprinkle the surface with the butter cut into chunks and place the baking pan inside the air fryer.
- Cook at 180 ° C for 20 minutes.
- After cooking, remove the baking pan from the air fryer.
- Divide the flan into 4 portions, put it on serving plates and serve.

Timbale of pasta with leeks

PREPARATION TIME: 25 minutes I COOKING TIME: 45 minutes I SERVINGS: 4

- ✓ 360 gr of fusilli
- ✓ 4 leeks
- ✓ 1 glass of white wine
- ✓ ½ glass of milk
- ✓ 2 eggs
- ✓ 80 gr of grated Parmesan cheese
- ✓ 6 sage leaves
- ✓ Butter to taste
- ✓ Olive oil to taste
- ✓ Salt and pepper to taste

DIRECTIONS

- ➢ Remove the white part of the leeks, wash them, and then cut them into thin slices.
- ➢ Put the leeks in a saucepan with a knob of butter and 50 ml of water and let them simmer slowly over low heat.
- ➢ Add the wine and let it evaporate.
- ➢ Pour in the milk and let it reduce. When the liquid has reduced, season with salt and pepper and turn off.
- ➢ Meanwhile, boil the fusilli in plenty of salted water for 5 minutes, then drain and put them in a bowl.
- ➢ Add the leeks and mix well.
- ➢ Brush a baking pan with olive oil and then pour the fusilli and leeks inside.
- ➢ Shell the eggs in a bowl and add the Parmesan.
- ➢ Mix well and then pour the mixture over the pasta.
- ➢ Wash and dry the sage and put it on top of the pasta together with the butter cut into chunks.
- ➢ Put the baking pan inside the fryer and cook at 180 ° C for 35 minutes.
- ➢ After cooking, remove the baking pan from the air fryer.
- ➢ Divide the pasta into 4 portions, put it on serving plates and serve.

Snacks and sides

Baskets of asparagus and bacon

PREPARATION TIME: 20 minutes I COOKING TIME: 26 minutes I SERVINGS: 4

- ✓ 400 gr of asparagus
- ✓ 1 roll of rectangular puff pastry
- ✓ 12 slices of bacon
- ✓ 100 gr of cheddar
- ✓ 1 clove of garlic
- ✓ Salt and pepper to taste
- ✓ Olive oil to taste

DIRECTIONS

- ➢ Peel and chop the garlic.
- ➢ Remove the asparagus stem and cut the tips into small pieces.
- ➢ Put the asparagus in a bowl and add salt, pepper, oil, and garlic and mix well.
- ➢ Put the asparagus in the air fryer and cook at 180 ° C for 10 minutes.
- ➢ Once cooked, take the asparagus, and place them on a plate.
- ➢ Put the puff pastry on a work surface and cut it into 4 x 5 cm rectangles.
- ➢ Put the rectangles in the muffin moulds brushed with olive oil.
- ➢ Place two slices of bacon, the sliced cheddar, and a little asparagus inside the puff pastry.
- ➢ Season with a little pepper and place the moulds inside the air fryer.
- ➢ Cook at 200 ° C for 16 minutes.
- ➢ After cooking, remove the muffin tins from the fryer and let them cool.

- Remove the baskets from the moulds, place them on serving plates and serve.

Chunks of salmon and bacon

PREPARATION TIME: 25 minutes I COOKING TIME: 10 minutes I SERVINGS: 4

- ✓ 800 gr of salmon fillet
- ✓ 150 gr of sliced bacon
- ✓ Sage leaves to taste
- ✓ Salt and pepper to taste
- ✓ Olive oil to taste

DIRECTIONS

- Wash and dry the salmon, remove the skin and bones, and then cut it into 2 cm cubes.
- Season the salmon with salt and pepper.
- Wash and dry the sage leaves (they must be the same number as the salmon cubes).
- Wrap the salmon and sage leaves with the bacon slices.
- Close the salmon and bacon morsels with toothpicks and place them inside the air fryer.
- Cook at 190 ° C for 10 minutes.
- Once cooked, remove the salmon bites from the air fryer, place them on plates and serve.

Courgette muffins

PREPARATION TIME: 25 minutes I COOKING TIME: 12 minutes I SERVINGS: 6

- ✓ 250 gr of flour
- ✓ 2 eggs
- ✓ 200 ml of milk
- ✓ 250 gr of courgettes
- ✓ 100 gr of cheddar
- ✓ 20 gr of toasted pine nuts
- ✓ 50 gr of grated Parmesan cheese
- ✓ 8 gr of instant yeast
- ✓ 50 ml of olive oil
- ✓ Salt and pepper to taste

DIRECTIONS

- Spike and peel the courgettes, wash them, and then grate them.
- Cut the cheddar into cubes.
- Shell the eggs in a bowl and then beat it with a hand whisk.
- Add the milk and oil and continue mixing.
- Pour in the flour and baking powder and mix until a homogeneous mixture is obtained.
- Now add the courgettes, cheddar and parmesan and mix again.
- Brush muffin moulds with olive oil and pour the mixture inside.
- Place the moulds inside the air fryer and cook at 180 ° C for 12 minutes.
- After cooking, remove the moulds from the air fryer.
- Allow to cool completely, then remove the muffins from the moulds and serve.

Crostini with flavoured feta

PREPARATION TIME: 20 minutes I REST TIME: 3 hours I COOKING TIME: 4 minutes I SERVINGS: 4

- ✓ 150 gr of feta
- ✓ 1 clove of garlic
- ✓ 1 anchovy in oil
- ✓ 4 basil leaves

- ✓ 1 tsp of dried oregano
- ✓ 1 tsp of chopped rosemary
- ✓ 1 tbsp of chopped parsley
- ✓ 250 gr of tomatoes
- ✓ 400 gr of bread
- ✓ Salt and pepper to taste
- ✓ Olive oil to taste

DIRECTIONS

- ➤ Chop the anchovy and put it in a bowl together with the oregano, parsley, and rosemary.
- ➤ Wash and dry the basil and then chop it.
- ➤ Peel the garlic and then chop it.
- ➤ Add the basil and garlic to the bowl with the other ingredients.
- ➤ Cut the feta into cubes, put it in the bowl with the herbs and season with oil, salt and pepper.
- ➤ Mix well, put the bowl in the fridge and marinate for 3 hours.
- ➤ After 3 hours, take the feta cheese from the fridge.
- ➤ Cut the bread into slices and then brush it with olive oil.
- ➤ Place the bread in the air fryer and bake at 180 ° C for two minutes per side.
- ➤ Meanwhile, wash the tomatoes and cut them into cubes, put them in a bowl and season with oil, salt and pepper.
- ➤ When the bread is ready, remove it from the air fryer and place it on the plates.
- ➤ Sprinkle the surface first with the tomato and then with the flavoured feta and serve.

Crostini with mushrooms

PREPARATION TIME: 10 minutes I COOKING TIME: 12 minutes I SERVINGS: 4

- ✓ 400 gr of bread
- ✓ 100 gr of cheddar
- ✓ 400 gr of champignon mushrooms
- ✓ 1 clove of garlic
- ✓ 1 tbsp of chopped parsley
- ✓ Salt and pepper to taste
- ✓ Olive oil to taste

DIRECTIONS

- ➤ Remove the final part of the mushrooms, wash them, dry them, and then cut them into slices.
- ➤ Peel the garlic and then chop it.
- ➤ Put the mushrooms and garlic in a bowl and add the parsley, salt, pepper, and oil and mix well.
- ➤ Put the mushrooms inside the air fryer and cook at 180 ° for 8 minutes.
- ➤ Once cooked, remove the mushrooms from the air fryer and set aside.
- ➤ Brush the bread with olive oil and place it inside the air fryer.
- ➤ Bake at 180 °C for 2 minutes, then turn the bread, put the sliced cheddar on top and cook for another 2 minutes.
- ➤ Once cooked, take the bread out of the air fryer, and place it on the plates.
- ➤ Sprinkle with the mushrooms and serve.

Herb and yogurt muffins

PREPARATION TIME: 20 minutes I COOKING TIME: 15 minutes I SERVINGS: 4280 gr of flour

- ✓ 8 gr of instant yeast for savoury pies
- ✓ 40 gr of cheddar
- ✓ 1 egg
- ✓ 200 gr of Greek yogurt
- ✓ 150 ml of milk
- ✓ 35 ml of olive oil

- ✓ 2 sprigs of thyme
- ✓ 1 tbsp of chopped parsley
- ✓ 2 sprigs of marjoram
- ✓ Salt and pepper to taste

DIRECTIONS

- ➤ Put the yogurt, milk, oil, and egg in a bowl and mix everything well.
- ➤ Wash and dry the thyme and marjoram and then chop them.
- ➤ Put the marjoram, thyme, and parsley in the bowl with the yogurt. Stir again and leave to flavour well.
- ➤ Put the flour, baking powder, salt, pepper, grated cheddar in another bowl and mix until you get a homogeneous mixture.
- ➤ Pour the flour mix into the bowl with the yogurt and mix well with a spatula until you get a homogeneous and lump-free mixture.
- ➤ Brush muffin moulds with olive oil and pour the mixture inside.
- ➤ Put the moulds in the air fryer and cook at 180 ° C for 15 minutes.
- ➤ Once cooked, remove the moulds, and let the muffins cool.
- ➤ When they have cooled, remove the muffins from the moulds and serve.

Mushroom, ham, and cheddar appetizers

PREPARATION TIME: 25 minutes I COOKING TIME: 17 minutes I SERVINGS: 4

- ✓ 1 roll of puff pastry
- ✓ 200 gr of champignon mushrooms
- ✓ 80 gr of raw ham
- ✓ 80 grams of cheddar

- ✓ 4 yolks
- ✓ Salt and pepper to taste
- ✓ Olive oil to taste

DIRECTIONS

- ➤ Remove the stem from the mushrooms, wash them under running water and pat them dry with a paper towel.
- ➤ Cut the mushrooms into thin slices, place them in the air fryer, and season with oil, salt, and pepper.
- ➤ Cook at 180 ° C for 5 minutes.
- ➤ Once cooked, take the mushrooms out of the air fryer, and set them aside.
- ➤ Roll out the puff pastry on a lightly floured work surface and, with the help of a 10 cm diameter pastry cutter, make 8 discs of dough.
- ➤ Spread a slice of ham on the surface of the pasta.
- ➤ Spread a little mushroom and a little cheddar on each disc, then close the dough on the filling.
- ➤ Seal the edges of the dough well and brush with beaten egg yolk.
- ➤ Place the dumplings inside the air fryer and cook at 200 ° C for 12 minutes.
- ➤ Once cooked, remove the bundles from the air fryer.
- ➤ Let it cool slightly then put the dumplings on the plates and serve.

Peppers cream

PREPARATION TIME: 20 minutes I COOKING TIME: 15 minutes I SERVINGS: 4

- ✓ 4 red peppers 4
- ✓ 2 tsp of paprika
- ✓ 2 tbsp of apple cider vinegar
- ✓ 12 mint leaves

- ✓ Salt and pepper to taste
- ✓ Olive oil to taste

DIRECTIONS

- ➢ Wash and dry the peppers, cut them in half and remove the stalk, seeds and white filaments.
- ➢ Put the peppers inside the air fryer and cook at 180 ° C for 15 minutes.
- ➢ Once cooked, remove them from the fryer, put them on a plate and let them cool.
- ➢ When they have cooled, remove the skin, and put them in a bowl.
- ➢ Wash and dry the mint leaves and place them in the bowl with the peppers.
- ➢ Season with vinegar, oil, salt, and pepper and then blend everything with an immersion blender.
- ➢ Divide the pepper cream into 4 bowls, season with a drizzle of oil and serve.

Plum and bacon rolls

PREPARATION TIME: 15 minutes I COOKING TIME: 4 minutes I SERVINGS: 4

- ✓ 12 dried plums
- ✓ 6 slices of bacon

DIRECTIONS

- ➢ Take the slices of bacon and divide them in half.
- ➢ Pitted the plums.
- ➢ Place a plum on each slice of bacon and then roll the bacon around the plum.
- ➢ At the end, keep the bacon and prunes closed with the help of a toothpick.
- ➢ Place the rolls inside the air fryer and cook at 180 ° C for 4 minutes, turning the rolls halfway through cooking.

- ➢ Once cooked, remove the rolls from the air fryer, place them on serving plates and serve.

Puff pastry with ham and spinach

PREPARATION TIME: 25 minutes I COOKING TIME: 15 minutes I SERVINGS: 4

- ✓ 1 roll of rectangular puff pastry
- ✓ 150 ml of béchamel
- ✓ 65 gr of sliced cooked ham
- ✓ 50 grams of cooked spinach
- ✓ 2 tbsp of grated Parmesan cheese
- ✓ 20 gr of grated Gruyere
- ✓ Salt and pepper to taste

DIRECTIONS

- ➢ Chop the cooked ham and put it in a bowl.
- ➢ Add the parmesan and béchamel and mix well.
- ➢ Chop the spinach and put them in the bowl with the ham and mix again.
- ➢ Cut the puff pastry into 8 squares of 12 cm each.
- ➢ Put a generous spoonful of filling in the centre of each pastry.
- ➢ Add the Gruyere and then fold the corners of the puff pastry towards the centre.
- ➢ Place the bundles inside the air fryer and cook at 200 ° C for 15 minutes.
- ➢ Once cooked, remove the bundles from the air fryer, place them on serving plates and serve.

Pumpkin chips

PREPARATION TIME: 20 minutes I COOKING TIME: 20 minutes I SERVNGS: 4

- ✓ 600 gr of pumpkin pulp
- ✓ 2 sprigs of rosemary
- ✓ 4 sage leaves
- ✓ Salt and pepper to taste
- ✓ Olive oil to taste

DIRECTIONS

- ➢ Wash and dry the pumpkin pulp and then cut it into slices about 2 cm thick.
- ➢ Wash and dry the sage and rosemary and chop them.
- ➢ Put the pumpkin slices in the air fryer, season them with salt, pepper and olive oil and then sprinkle them with the aromatic herbs.
- ➢ Close the air fryer and cook at 180°C for 20 minutes, turning the pumpkin halfway through cooking.
- ➢ Once cooked, remove the pumpkin from the air fryer and let it rest for 10 minutes.
- ➢ Now put the pumpkin chips on the serving plates and serve.

Rustic with herbs and cheese

PREPARATION TIME: 20 minutes I COOKING TIME: 12 minutes I SERVINGS: 4

- ✓ 1 roll of rectangular puff pastry
- ✓ 250 gr of fresh mixed chopped herbs
- ✓ 150 gr of fresh spreadable cheese
- ✓ Sultana grapes to taste
- ✓ Salt and pepper to taste
- ✓ Olive oil to taste

DIRECTIONS

- ➢ Put the spreadable cheese in a bowl and add the herbs, salt, pepper, a little oil and the sultanas.
- ➢ Mix until you get a homogeneous mixture.
- ➢ Divide the puff pastry in two and brush the filling of one half of the pastry.
- ➢ Cover with the other half and then cut it into cubes.
- ➢ Put the puff pastry cubes inside the air fryer and cook them at 180 ° C for 12 minutes.
- ➢ Once cooked, remove the rustic from the air fryer and place them on a serving dish.
- ➢ Let it cool and then serve.

Savoury muffins with olives

PREPARATION TIME: 20 minutes I COOKING TIME: 12 minutes I SERVINGS: 4

- ✓ 100 gr of flour of
- ✓ 1 egg
- ✓ 3 gr of instant yeast
- ✓ 25 ml of olive oil
- ✓ 25 ml of seed oil
- ✓ 20 gr of peeled almonds
- ✓ 60 ml of milk
- ✓ 6 pitted green olives
- ✓ 6 pitted black olives
- ✓ 1 tbsp of chopped thyme
- ✓ 1 tsp of sugar
- ✓ Salt and pepper to taste

DIRECTIONS

- ➢ Put the almonds, thyme, milk, egg, and olives in the blender.

- Operate the mixer and blend until a homogeneous mixture is obtained.
- Put the mixture in a bowl and add the flour, yeast, sugar, a pinch of salt and pepper.
- Mix everything well until the mixture is homogeneous and free of lumps.
- Put the cups inside the muffin moulds and then divide the mixture inside.
- Cook at 180 ° C for 12 minutes.
- Once cooked, remove the moulds, and let the muffins cool.
- When they are cold enough, remove the muffins from the moulds and serve.

Sweet potato chips

PREPARATION TIME: 20 minutes I COOKING TIME: 10 minutes I SERVINGS: 4

- ✓ 4 sweet potatoes
- ✓ 1 tsp of sweet paprika
- ✓ 2 sprigs of thyme
- ✓ Olive oil to taste
- ✓ Salt and pepper to taste

DIRECTIONS

- Wash and dry the thyme and then chop it.
- Put the thyme in a bowl and add the paprika, oil, salt, and pepper.
- Mix well and keep the emulsion aside.
- Wash the potatoes thoroughly under running water, dry them and then cut them into thin slices.
- Brush the potato slices with the emulsion and then place them inside the air fryer.
- Cook at 200 ° C for 10 minutes, turning the potatoes halfway through cooking.

- Once cooked, remove the sweet potato chips from the air fryer, divide them into serving plates and serve.

Tofu meatballs

PREPARATION TIME: 20 minutes I COOKING TIME: 8 minutes I SERVINGS: 4

- ✓ 250 grams of tofu
- ✓ 50 gr of breadcrumbs
- ✓ 30 grams of flour
- ✓ 12 sage leaves
- ✓ 50 gr of rolled oats
- ✓ Salt and pepper to taste
- ✓ Olive oil to taste

DIRECTIONS

- Dab the tofu with a paper towel and place it in a bowl.
- Wash the sage leaves, chop them, and put them in the bowl with the tofu.
- Add the flour, breadcrumbs, salt, and pepper and mix everything well.
- Knead the mixture by first mashing it with a fork, then squeezing it in your hands, so that no lumps remain and the flour melts perfectly.
- Start forming the meatballs by taking a small amount of the mixture and rolling it in your hands.
- Put the oat flakes on a plate and pass the meatballs on top.
- Put the meatballs in the air fryer and sprinkle some oil on the surface.
- Cook at 180 ° C for 8 minutes, turning them halfway through cooking and sprinkling more olive oil.
- Once cooked, remove the meatballs from the air fryer, place them on serving plates and serve.

Desserts and sweets

Almond and apricot cake

PREPARATION TIME: 25 minutes I COOKING TIME: 30 minutes I SERVINGS: 8/10

- ✓ 200 gr of butter
- ✓ 4 small eggs
- ✓ 250 gr of flour
- ✓ 5 gr of instant yeast for sweets
- ✓ 100 gr of almond flour
- ✓ 250 ml of milk
- ✓ 80 ml of honey
  1 tsp of cinnamon powder
- ✓ 10 apricots
- ✓ sliced almonds to taste
- ✓ 1 pinch of salt

DIRECTIONS

- ➢ Put the butter cut into small pieces in a bowl and work it with an electric mixer until you get a creamy mixture.
- ➢ Add the eggs, one at a time, waiting for the first to incorporate well before adding the other.
- ➢ Add the flour, almond flour, milk, and honey, continuing to mix until you get a homogeneous and lump-free mixture.
- ➢ Finally add the cinnamon and salt and finish mixing.
- ➢ Wash the apricots, cut them in half and remove the stone.
- ➢ Brush a baking pan with olive oil and put the mixture inside.
- ➢ Place the apricots and sliced almonds on top and put the baking pan in the air fryer.
- ➢ Cook at 180 ° C for 30 minutes.

- ➢ Finish cooking, remove the baking pan from the air fryer and let it cool.
- ➢ Turn the cake upside down on a serving dish, cut into slices and serve.

Berries crumble

PREPARATION TIME: 25 minutes I COOKING TIME: 40 minutes I SERVINGS: 4

- ✓ 200 gr of flour
- ✓ 500 gr of berries
- ✓ 10 gr of potato starch
- ✓ 70 gr of softened butter
- ✓ 1 lemon
- ✓ 80 gr of granulated sugar
- ✓ 50 gr of brown sugar
- ✓ 50 gr of sliced almonds

DIRECTIONS

- ➢ Wash the berries and put them in a pot.
- ➢ Add the granulated sugar and the potato starch.
- ➢ Add the lemon juice and bring to a boil.
- ➢ Arrange the fruit in a baking pan and level the surface using a spatula.
- ➢ Put the butter cut into chunks and put it in the bowl.
- ➢ Add the brown sugar and whisk with an electric mixer until you get a light and fluffy mixture.
- ➢ Add the flour a little at a time and continue to whip the dough quickly.
- ➢ When it has reached a sandy consistency, put the mixture on the berries.
- ➢ Sprinkle the sliced almonds on top and place the baking pan inside the air fryer.
- ➢ Cook at 190 ° C for 30 minutes. After 30 minutes, check the cooking and, if the surface is not golden brown, continue cooking for another 5 minutes.

- After cooking, remove the baking pan from the air fryer.
- Let it cool for 15 minutes, then cut it into slices, put it on serving plates and serve.

Carrots pie

PREPARATION TIME: 25 minutes I COOKING TIME: 35 minutes I SERVINGS: 8/10

- ✓ 300 gr of flour
- ✓ 100 gr of almond flour
- ✓ 150 gr of sugar
- ✓ 300 gr of peeled carrots
- ✓ 100 ml of seed oil
- ✓ 4 small eggs
- ✓ 1 orange
- ✓ 1 tsp of vanilla essence
- ✓ 10 gr of baking powder
- ✓ 1 pinch of salt

DIRECTIONS

- Wash the carrots and then cut them into small pieces.
- Put the carrots in the mixer and chop finely.
- Put the carrots in a bowl and add the flour, baking powder and almond flour.
- Stir until you get a homogeneous mixture.
- Wash the orange and grate the zest.
- Shell the eggs in a bowl and add the sugar, salt, vanilla, and orange zest.
- Whip with an electric mixer, until you get a light and fluffy mixture.
- Add the flour mix and mix well.
- Finally, add the oil and continue whipping until you get a smooth and lump-free mixture.
- Brush a baking pan with olive oil and put the mixture inside.

- Cook at 170 ° C for 35 minutes.
- After cooking, remove the baking pan from the fryer and let the cake cool completely.
- When the cake is cold, remove it from the pan and place it on a serving dish.
- Sprinkle the cake with icing sugar, cut into slices and serve.

Chocolate plumcake

PREPARATION TIME: 25 minutes I COOKING TIME: 35 minutes I SERVINGS: 8/10

- ✓ 180 gr of butter softened at room temperature
- ✓ 180 gr of brown sugar
- ✓ 150 gr of dark chocolate
- ✓ 50 gr of honey
- ✓ 50 ml of milk
- ✓ 6 large eggs
- ✓ 8 gr of brewer's yeast
- ✓ 300 gr of flour
- ✓ 150 gr of chocolate chips
- ✓ 1 pinch of baking soda

DIRECTIONS

- Put the dark chocolate in a saucepan and melt it in a bain-marie.
- Cut the butter into chunks and put it in a bowl.
- Add the sugar and whisk with an electric mixer until you get a fluffy and smooth mixture.
- Add the melted chocolate and continue mixing.
- Add the honey and baking soda and mix again.
- Then add the eggs, one at a time and stir until they are completely incorporated into the mixture.

- ➤ Then add the milk and flour, alternating them, and mix until you get a smooth and lump-free mixture.
- ➤ Finally, add the chocolate chips and mix well.
- ➤ Brush a plumcake mould with olive oil and pour the mixture inside.
- ➤ Put the mould inside the air fryer and cook at 180 ° C for 35 minutes.
- ➤ After cooking, remove the mould from the fryer and let it cool.
- ➤ When the plum cake is warm, remove it from the mould and place it on a dessert plate.
- ➤ Cut the plum cake into slices, put it on plates and serve.

Clafoutis with apples

PREPARATION TIME: 25 minutes I COOKING TIME: 25 minutes I SERVINGS: 4

- ✓ 4 medium apples
- ✓ 250 ml of milk
- ✓ 2 eggs
- ✓ 1 lemon
- ✓ 160 gr of sugar
- ✓ 20 gr of butter
- ✓ 150 gr of flour

DIRECTIONS

- ➤ Peel the apples, remove the seeds and core, and then cut them into slices.
- ➤ Put the apples in a bowl and add the lemon juice.
- ➤ Stir and leave to flavour for 15 minutes.
- ➤ Meanwhile, shell the eggs and separate the yolks from the whites.
- ➤ Beat the egg whites until stiff.
- ➤ Mix the egg yolks with the sugar until you get a light and fluffy mixture.

- ➤ Add the milk and flour and continue mixing until you get a homogeneous and lump-free mixture.
- ➤ Add the egg whites and mix from the bottom up until they are completely incorporated.
- ➤ Brush a round cake pan with melted butter and pour the mixture.
- ➤ Put the apples on top of the dough and place the pan inside the air fryer.
- ➤ Cook at 180 ° C for 25 minutes.
- ➤ Always check the cooking and, if it is not yet cooked, continue for another 5 minutes.
- ➤ After cooking, remove the cake pan from the air fryer.
- ➤ Let the clafoutis cool, then turn it upside down on a serving dish for desserts.
- ➤ Sprinkle with sugar and icing, cut the clafoutis into slices and serve.

Lemon and walnut plumcake

PREPARATION TIME: 20 minutes I COOKING TIME: 25 minutes I SERVINGS: 8/10

- ✓ 300 gr of flour
- ✓ 150 gr of sugar
- ✓ 1 tsp of instant yeast for cakes
- ✓ 2 large eggs
- ✓ 100 gr of butter softened at room temperature
- ✓ 100 ml of milk
- ✓ 100 gr of walnuts
- ✓ 1 lemon
- ✓ A pinch of baking soda

DIRECTIONS

- ➢ Cut the butter into chunks and put it in a bowl with the sugar.
- ➢ Whip the butter and sugar with an electric mixer, until you get a frothy and homogeneous mixture.
- ➢ Add the eggs, flour and baking powder and continue mixing.
- ➢ Wash and dry the lemon and grate the zest into the bowl with the mixture.
- ➢ Chop the walnuts and put them in the mixture.
- ➢ Finally add the milk and mix well until you get a homogeneous mixture.
- ➢ Brush a plumcake mould with olive oil and pour the mixture inside.
- ➢ Put the mould inside the air fryer.
- ➢ Cook at 180°C for 25 minutes.
- ➢ Check the cooking with a toothpick and, if it is not yet cooked, continue for another 5 minutes.
- ➢ After cooking, remove the mould from the fryer.
- ➢ Let the plumcake cool, then place it on a serving dish for desserts.
- ➢ Cut the plumcake into slices, put it on plates and serve.

Lemon bars

PREPARATION TIME: 30 minutes I COOKING TIME: 30 minutes I SERVINGS: 8

- ✓ 200 gr of flour
- ✓ 70 gr of powdered sugar
- ✓ 100 gra of butter softened at room temperature
- ✓ 150 grams of granulated sugar
- ✓ 2 eggs
- ✓ ½ lemon

DIRECTIONS

- ➢ Mix the flour and butter in a bowl at room temperature.
- ➢ Then add the icing sugar.
- ➢ Knead as if you were making a shortcrust pastry, using a few tablespoons of cold water, if necessary.
- ➢ Knead until you get a homogeneous mixture.
- ➢ Form the mixture into a ball and let it rest in the fridge for 30 minutes.
- ➢ When the dough is ready, roll it out with a rolling pin.
- ➢ Line a square cake pans with the dough.
- ➢ Put the cake pan in the air fryer and cook at 180 ° C for 15 minutes.
- ➢ Meanwhile, prepare the cream.
- ➢ Shell the eggs in a bowl and separate the yolks from the whites.
- ➢ Whip the egg yolks together with the granulated sugar, then add the rest of the flour and the lemon juice.
- ➢ Set it aside (without cooking it).
- ➢ When you have taken the base out of the oven, pour the cream over it and put it back inside the air fryer.
- ➢ Continue cooking for another 15 minutes.
- ➢ After cooking, remove the cake pan from the air fryer and let it cool completely.
- ➢ Cut the cake into squares and sprinkle with icing sugar.

Lemon chiffon cake

PREPARATION TIME: 25 minutes I COOKING TIME: 45 minutes I SERVINGS:8/10

- ✓ 300 gr of flour
- ✓ 4 medium eggs
- ✓ 200 gr of sugar
- ✓ 150 ml of lemon juice

- ✓ 1 lemon
- ✓ 100 ml of warm water
- ✓ 80 ml of seed oil
- ✓ 8 gr of instant yeast for sweets
- ✓ 1 pinch of salt
- ✓ 4 gr of cream of tartar

DIRECTIONS

- ➤ Wash the lemon and grate the zest in a bowl.
- ➤ Add the flour, salt and baking powder and mix well.
- ➤ Put the lemon juice, water and seed oil in another bowl and mix well.
- ➤ Shell the eggs and put the egg whites and cream of tartar in a bowl and then whisk them until stiff.
- ➤ Put the egg yolks in the bowl with the liquid ingredients and mix again until they are completely incorporated.
- ➤ Incorporate the flour into the liquid components. Stir until you get a homogeneous and lump-free mixture.
- ➤ Brush a chiffon cake mould with olive oil and pour the mixture inside.
- ➤ Put the mould inside the air fryer and cook at 170 ° C for 45 minutes.
- ➤ After cooking, remove the mould from the air fryer and let the chiffon cake cool.
- ➤ When it is cold, turn it upside down on a serving dish.
- ➤ Sprinkle with icing sugar, cut the chiffon cake into slices and serve.

Lemon drizzle cake

PREPARATION TIME: 30 minutes I COOKING TIME: 35 minutes I SERVINGS: 8/10

- ✓ 200 gr of flour
- ✓ 120 gr of sugar

- ✓ 100 gr of softened butter
- ✓ 2 large eggs
- ✓ 50 ml of milk
- ✓ The grated zest of one lemon
- ✓ 1 tsp of baking powder
- ✓ For the lemon syrup:
- ✓ 1 lemon
- ✓ 1 tbsp of sugar
- ✓ 4 tbsp of powdered sugar

DIRECTIONS

- ➤ Cut the butter into chunks and put it in a bowl.
- ➤ Add the sugar and whisk with an electric mixer until you get a thick and creamy mixture.
- ➤ Add the egg and continue to whip the mixture.
- ➤ Add the flour, baking powder and grated lemon zest.
- ➤ Mix well and finally add the milk.
- ➤ Stir until you get a smooth, lump-free mixture.
- ➤ Brush a round cake pan with olive oil and pour the mixture inside.
- ➤ Place the cake pan inside the air fryer and cook at 180 ° C for 35 minutes.
- ➤ Meanwhile, make the lemon syrup.
- ➤ Wash and dry the lemon and remove the zest.
- ➤ Put the icing sugar in a bowl and add the lemon juice.
- ➤ Stir until you get a homogeneous mixture.
- ➤ Pour the mixture into a saucepan and heat it, without bringing it to a boil.
- ➤ Chop the lemon zest and mix it with the sugar.
- ➤ Once cooked, remove the cake from the air fryer.

- Let the cake cool and then remove it from the pan.
- Make small holes on the surface of the cake and then pour over the syrup.
- Sprinkle with the lemon sugar, cut the cake into slices and serve.

Madeira cake

PREPARATION TIME: 15 minutes I COOKING TIME: 40 minutes I SERVINGS: 8/10

- ✓ 100 gr of softened butter
- ✓ 200 gr of sugar
- ✓ 300 gr of flour
- ✓ 4 small eggs
- ✓ 10 gr of baking powder
- ✓ 1 lemon
- ✓ 1 vanilla bean
- ✓ 1 pinch of salt

DIRECTIONS

- Cut the butter into chunks and put it in a bowl with the sugar.
- Add the vanilla bean and whisk them with an electric mixer.
- When you have obtained a creamy mixture, add 1 whole egg at a time alternating it with a tablespoon of flour.
- Add the baking powder, salt, and the rest of the flour and continue mixing.
- Wash and dry the lemon, grate the zest, and strain the juice into the bowl with the mixture.
- Stir until you get a smooth, lump-free mixture.
- Brush the baking pan with olive oil and pour the mixture inside.
- Place the baking pan in the air fryer and cook at 160 ° C for 40 minutes.

- After cooking, remove the baking pan from the air fryer.
- Let the cake cool completely and then remove them from the pan.
- Put the cake on a dessert plate.
- Sprinkle the cake with icing sugar, cut into slices and serve.

Orange and cranberry cake

PREPARATION TIME: 30 minutes I COOKING TIME: 35 minutes I SERVINGS: 8/10

- ✓ 300 grams of flour
- ✓ 4 small eggs
- ✓ 2 egg whites
- ✓ 50 gr of powdered sugar
- ✓ 1 tsp of cinnamon powder
- ✓ 200 gr of cranberries
- ✓ 100 gr of melted butter
- ✓ 150 ml of milk
- ✓ 120 gr of granulated sugar
- ✓ 8 gr of instant yeast for sweets
- ✓ 2 oranges

DIRECTIONS

- Shell the eggs in a bowl and add the sugar. Beat them with an electric mixer until the mixture is light and fluffy.
- Add the melted butter and stir until completely incorporated.
- Add the flour and baking powder, alternating them with the milk.
- Wash and dry the orange, grate, and strain the juice into the bowl with the mixture.
- Stir until you get a smooth, lump-free mixture.
- Pour in the cranberries and finish mixing.

- Brush a baking pan with olive oil and pour the mixture inside.
- Put the baking pan inside the air fryer and cook at 180 ° C for 35 minutes.
- Meanwhile, make the cinnamon glaze. Put the egg white and whip it with the icing sugar and cinnamon until the mixture is smooth and not too liquid.
- Once the cake is cooked, take the baking pan out of the air fryer and let it cool.
- Divide the cake into three layers and sprinkle the surface of each with the cinnamon glaze.
- Now cut the cake into slices and serve.

Peach and apricot crumble

PREPARATION TIME: 25 minutes I COOKING TIME: 25 minutes I SERVINGS: 4

- ✓ 350 gr of peaches
- ✓ 250 gr of apricots
- ✓ 150 gr of flour
- ✓ 60 gr of brown sugar
- ✓ 85 gr of butter
- ✓ 2 tbsp of sliced almonds
- ✓ 1 lemon
- ✓ 1 pinch of salt

DIRECTIONS

- Peel the peaches, remove the stone, and then cut them into cubes.
- Wash the apricots, remove the stones, and then cut them into cubes.
- Put the apricots and peaches in a bowl and add 10 g of sugar and lemon juice.
- Mix well and leave to macerate for 15 minutes.

- Put the flour, the salt, the rest of the sugar and the butter cut into chunks in another bowl.
- Work the ingredients with your hands until you get a sandy mixture.
- Brush a baking pan with olive oil and then put the fruit inside.
- Add the dough to the surface and place the baking pan inside the air fryer.
- Cook at 180 ° C for 25 minutes.
- After cooking, remove the baking pan from the air fryer and let it cool for 10 minutes.
- After 10 minutes, cut the crumble into slices, put it on serving plates and serve.

Peanut Butter Cake

PREPARATION TIME: 25 minutes I COOKING TIME: 25 minutes I SERVINGS: 8/10

- ✓ 150 gr of granulated sugar
- ✓ 80 gr of peanut butter
- ✓ 4 small eggs
- ✓ 80 gr of softened butter
- ✓ 300 gr of flour
- ✓ 200 ml of milk
- ✓ 80 gr of chocolate chips
- ✓ 50 gr of potato starch
- ✓ 8 gr of instant baking powder
- ✓ 1 pinch of baking soda

DIRECTIONS

- Put the chopped butter, sugar, and peanut butter in a bowl.
- Whip with an electric whisk until you get a smooth and creamy mixture.
- Now add an egg, stir and when it is incorporated, add the second.
- Add the flour, starch and yeast alternating them with the milk.

- ➢ Finally add the chocolate chips and baking soda and mix until you get a homogeneous mixture.
- ➢ Brush a baking pan with olive oil and pour the mixture inside.
- ➢ Put the baking pan inside the air fryer and cook at 180 ° for 25 minutes.
- ➢ After cooking, remove the baking pan from the air fryer.
- ➢ Let the cake cool and then pour it into a dessert plate.
- ➢ Cut the cake into slices, put it on plates and serve.

Plumcake with blueberries and orange

PREPARATION TIME: 25 minutes I COOKING TIME: 45 minutes I SERVINGS: 8/10

- ✓ 300 gr of flour
- ✓ 8 gr of instant yeast
- ✓ 125 gr of plain yogurt
- ✓ 1 tsp of vanilla essence
- ✓ 3 large eggs
- ✓ 150 gr of sugar
- ✓ 80 ml of olive oil
- ✓ 2 oranges
- ✓ 300 gr of blueberries

DIRECTIONS

- ➢ Wash and dry the orange, grate the zest, and strain the juice into a bowl.
- ➢ Put the orange zest in a bowl with the flour, baking powder and vanilla.
- ➢ Mix everything with a spatula.
- ➢ Shell the eggs in another bowl.
- ➢ Add the sugar and whisk with an electric mixer, until you get a light and fluffy mixture.

- ➢ Add the orange juice, yogurt and oil and mix until you get a homogeneous mixture.
- ➢ Now add the flour mix and mix again, until you get a lump-free mixture.
- ➢ Wash and dry the blueberries and put them in the bowl with the mixture.
- ➢ Stir and then pour the mixture into a plumcake mould brushed with olive oil.
- ➢ Put the mould inside the air fryer and cook at 180 ° for 45 minutes.
- ➢ Always check the cooking with a toothpick before finishing cooking.
- ➢ As soon as the plumcake is ready, remove the mould from the air fryer.
- ➢ Let the plumcake cool and then put it on a serving dish for desserts.
- ➢ Sprinkle with icing sugar, cut the plum cake into slices and serve.

Strawberry Crumble

PREPARATION TIME: 25 minutes I COOKING TIME: 20 minutes I SERVINGS: 4

- ✓ 400 gr of strawberries
- ✓ 60 gr of brown sugar
- ✓ 70 gr of cold butter
- ✓ 100 gr of flour
- ✓ 2 tbsp of chopped hazelnuts
- ✓ 1 tbsp of lemon juice

DIRECTIONS

- ➢ Wash and dry the strawberries, cut them in half and put them in a bowl.
- ➢ Add a tablespoon of brown sugar and lemon juice and mix.
- ➢ Put the flour in another bowl and add the butter cut into chunks.
- ➢ Knead the mixture until you get a sandy mixture.

- ➢ Add the remaining sugar and the chopped hazelnuts and knead again with your hands.
- ➢ Put the strawberries on the bottom of a cake pan.
- ➢ Put the dough on top and place the cake pan inside the air fryer.
- ➢ Cook at 180°C for 20 minutes.
- ➢ After cooking, remove the pan from the air fryer.
- ➢ Let it cool for 10 minutes, then cut the crumble into slices, put it on plates and serve.

Printed in Great Britain
by Amazon

10219567R00052